MONUMENTS

Embracing God's Desire and Design for Your Life

JOHN SHERRILL

Monuments
Embracing God's Desire and Design for Your Life

Published by Reflek Publishing
Design Concept: Melody Gathright / Unboxed Creative

Disclaimer: The author makes no guarantees concerning the level of success you may experience by following the advice and strategies contained in this book, and you accept the risk that results will differ for each individual. The purpose of this book is to educate, entertain, and inspire.

For more information: Hello@johnsherrill.com

ISBN: 978-1-968164-15-7 (paperback)
ISBN: 978-1-968164-16-4 (ebook)

For Kel, my love, who embodies and exemplifies the monumental God-saturated life in every way—you are my best friend and my now and forever.

And for my boys, Jadon, Jack, and Kyle—
this book is more than a mere collection of words to and for you;
it is a lifetime of stacked stones that I pray will stand
as an Ebenezer for you and your children.

Chloe girl, it's a good gift from God to have you as a daughter.
We are so thankful that He brought you and Jadon together.

A NOTE FROM JOHN

We are all on a journey, and my prayer is that, as I continue to go and grow, I won't miss out on anything God has for me or my family, and that I will continue to walk in a posture of wonder and willingness. I have not yet arrived, nor do I believe I ever will, until the day my faith is made sight. So until then, I continue to joyfully count myself among the tribe of wide-eyed, Spirit-filled, presence-hungry ragamuffins whose deepest desire in this life is to honor Jesus and make an indelible, eternal difference.

This book has been a lifetime in waiting, trusting God's timing in the invitation to finally put pen to paper. However, my hope is that these words, saturated by the Scriptures and based largely on experimentation in the lab room of life, will echo on for generations to come. I trust that God will use this effort to encourage somebody on their journey of embracing and living the abundant life God desires and has designed for them.

I believe God has good plans in mind for you, plans He dreamed for your life long before He spoke creation into existence. Therefore, my greatest joy is the idea that God may use me and my story, in some way, to fan the flames of your faith.

God is building a monument composed of His very own people, and I believe you and I are a part of that! May God use this book not only to inspire you but also to catalyze you to step into the dream and destiny that He created exclusively for you! Please know this: You are ONE OF ONE! You are the only one of You in all of God's creation. Your life deeply matters to God and to this world! You are a living declaration of the goodness of God, a memorial which points to His magnificence, and a monument that will echo with eternal impact.

May God bless you as He invites you into deeper places, engages you with bigger vision, and anoints you for His great purposes!

TABLE OF CONTENTS

INTRODUCTION

Psalm 148:13–14 (MSG)

Let them praise the name of GOD—it's
the only Name worth praising.

His radiance exceeds anything in earth and sky;

He's built a monument—His very own people!

The Origin of Monuments

Our world is full of monuments. Every standing memorial is specifically placed to commemorate a significant moment in time and tell a story worthy of remembrance. We learn of the first recorded monument in history in the book of Genesis. At the age of six hundred years old, God had a specific plan calling Noah to a significant purpose. To the world around him, I'm sure what Noah was doing seemed ludicrous. *Why are you building a boat, old man, especially a boat so large? Who needs a 450-foot-long, 75-foot-wide, and 45-foot-high yacht?*

It's quite possible the people around Noah thought he had gone mad, but the world rarely knows or can appreciate the lengths God will go to resurrect, restore, and redeem His creation. After the waters rose and fell, flooding the earth and bringing to death all living things, Noah and his family, as well as all the animals God had assigned him, survived. Not only did they survive, but God provided for their every need.

Building a huge monstrosity of a boat under clear blue skies may have seemed crazy to most, but to Noah and his family, it was a commission from God that required faith and obedience. When God calls and commissions people to His purposes, it can appear crazy to the world, but He is always deeply intentional and radically faithful, especially through the obedience and faith of the one He calls.

—

When God calls and commissions people to His purposes, it can appear crazy to the world, but He is always deeply intentional and radically faithful.

Finally, after nearly a year, God finished what He set out to accomplish, and Noah and his family were able to step out of God's vessel of protection onto dry land once again. It's here that we see Noah's first action after leaving the ark. Being a righteous, blameless man who always walked closely with God, the first thing Noah did after departing the boat was to build an altar of remembrance, memorializing the moment. Noah could clearly see that, through every terrifying moment over the last year of their lives, God had protected him and his family from the raging storm and had revealed Himself in powerful, beautiful, and meaningful ways.

At this monument, Noah burned offerings to the Lord and worshipped Him for His goodness and for the great things He had done. God, being pleased with Noah's faith and obedience, made a covenant with Noah at that moment and in that place.

Today, monuments are in abundance, yet very few are built in remembrance of the Lord. Our culture memorializes many people, places, and things for all sorts of reasons. People did the same back in Biblical times. Many monuments have been built to many things, including to false gods, in every generation. Our world loves commemorating things, building altars to lesser gods, and giving attention and allegiance to unworthy people, but God is more interested in building a different sort of monument.

He wants to build monuments to honor His name and commemorate His faithfulness—not carved from physical stone, but living monuments.

A Different Type of Monument

He was given less than a 1 percent chance of living, with a 0 percent chance of a normal quality of life if he somehow survived.

The birth of Kyle, my third son, was full of trauma. His skin wasn't fully formed, his eyes weren't open, he battled a clot in his heart, and, to make matters even worse, he developed a horrific brain bleed. On a scale from 1 to 4, with 4 being the worst, Kyle struggled with a grade 3 bleed on one side of his brain and a grade 4 on the other.

The odds were against us in every way, according to all the experts, and the volume of their voices kept growing louder. Turns out, when you're born prematurely at slightly over twenty-three weeks, you don't come out as the "cute" version of a preemie one might imagine. No, my son's entrance into the world was immediately a chaotic and radical ride full of doctors, diagnosis after diagnosis, delirium, and day after day of doing our best to keep believing with what most would call crazy faith—even in the face of crippling fear.

I became well acquainted with this Biblical statement: "Lord, I believe; help my unbelief." To be honest, there's far more to Kyle's story than I can share here, but over the next many weeks while his underdeveloped little body was struggling for life, God would loudly reveal many incredible and profound truths to countless people, beginning with my wife and me.

Truths like this: Every person God creates is created *on* purpose and *for* purpose. Our lives have deep meaning, genuinely matter, and will represent something. And finally, we were born for significance, and we all have a story to tell.

While our lives really aren't the point of God's greater story, we are a significant part of that story. What greater story am I speaking of? I'm talking about the story that God is writing in, about, and through your life. You are created in His image and for His glory, and He is deeply invested in the story your life is telling (and will tell).

A Divine Interruption

There is no possible or plausible way that our existence is the result of some cosmic, catalytic accident. The origins of this world didn't just "happen." It takes far more faith to believe that such intricate detail evolved from an explosion rather than from the design and hand of an intelligent Creator.

Make no mistake: Your life is not an accident or happenstance. We are wisely informed in Paul's words in the book of Colossians that we were made by God, through God, and for God. Of all the things He created, God made us to be image bearers. Simply put, our lives come from an intentional, creative, loving God who eternally desires us, then designed and formed us to become exactly who we are, because that's what He wanted.

—

Every person God creates is created on purpose and for purpose.

Kyle was no different. His entrance into this world had divine purpose and was a divine interruption. Did I have a million questions about why my son's story had to begin the way it did? Of course! Would I wish this sort of violent entrance on anyone? Absolutely not! Not far from my son's NICU room stood one of the largest Planned Parenthood abortion mills in the entire northern hemisphere at the time—a place that would never admit that my son was human or viable. I wondered, *God, what could You possibly want with this scenario? God, where are You? God, can You see this? God, why does this have to be my kid's story? God, what could You perhaps be doing in this?*

There I was, ten years deep into being a professional Christian. I was traveling, teaching, and leading worship for many different events, doing my best to make a living and make a difference. I spent a lot of time, energy, and money recording music, hosting conferences, and making myself available to be God's mouthpiece—however, wherever, and whenever possible. Kyle's birth was like hitting a concrete wall as we were going one hundred miles per hour down what felt like a highway of blessing.

Everything stopped.

The clear blue skies of our life quickly turned cloudy and dark from chaos and confusion. The only thing we had capacity for was survival: survival for Kyle, survival for our other two boys at home, survival for our marriage—just survival. At that moment, if I'm honest, it was infuriating to consider what God might be doing. As I waited, watched, and wept, all I could do was beg God to make a way where there seemed to be no way. I struggled deeply. I couldn't find that confidence that Kyle would be okay. I felt betrayed by God, and I felt left alone. What was once seemingly so easy had devolved into a dark season of deep insecurity, which led to even deeper feelings of insignificance.

The helplessness I felt suffocated any feelings of prior achievement or ministry fulfillment, because I could do nothing to impact the outcome in any way. I couldn't "will" my son to live, and I couldn't say or do anything to make sense of the scenario or bring peace to my wife and family. I couldn't force God's hand, nor would I dare try. As much as I feared what was to come, I revered God more. And while I would never want to go back and revisit that season of my life, I can tell you now, nearly eighteen years later, that God has used the story of my son more times than I can count to remind people of His promises and provision.

—

Your life is not an accident or happenstance.

This experience brought my family a greater depth to our faith in ways nothing else could, while revealing God's power, purpose, and plan for redeeming every situation and circumstance in our lives.

What About You?

Here's what I want you to hear me say: You matter. You are significant. God created you because He wanted to. He intentionally designed you just how you are and set you in the storyboard of time exactly when He wanted to. It's for such a time as this that you exist. Your life will represent something, and you have a story to tell!

Since we are all created in the image of God, to be God's image bearers, the most remarkable stories we can tell are those that point to Him and His goodness in how we live. We have a unique privilege that nothing else in all of creation has, not even the angelic beings. We have the privilege to live as a memorial to God's greatness, faithfulness, and power. God desires to use our surrendered and submitted lives to declare who He is to a wondering, watching, and waiting world around us. We can live a monumental life and leave behind a legacy worth writing about.

So let me ask you some questions:

- Have you ever felt insignificant and invisible?
- Have you ever wondered if your life will have any real meaning or if it will matter in any significant way?
- Will you ever make any sort of considerable mark in this world?
- Is it possible for there to be any real sense of legacy you leave behind after you're gone?

I only ask these questions because I've had to wrestle with them myself.

Living the Message Out Loud

It wasn't but a few minutes after my son was born that the news began to break. My phone started ringing. Over the next 115 days in the hospital, it rarely let up. Well-wishers from all over the country and around the world began to reach out. Even though the calls were occasionally encouraging, it all became a bit too overwhelming. We were doing our best to navigate through the valley of the shadow of death, and we couldn't keep up with people *and* our pain.

Social media wasn't yet the rage at that time (I know: I'm old), but the web was ripe with blogs. We were introduced to a platform called CaringBridge, so we began to update people through that medium. Whoever created CaringBridge should win a medal (and be filthy rich by now). It became a lifeline for us.

Soon, the drummer in my band, who is a good friend and was also savvy in web design, created a simple webpage with a memorable URL for our blog. In seemingly no time we discovered we had over 400,000 unique visitors to our blog, despite it being nothing but our medical updates, a few family musings to keep our boys in focus, and, at times, our prayers of desperation.

—

Your life will represent something, and you have a story to tell!

I want to be clear: We weren't trying to build a blog or a brand. This crisis was in no way a new initiative of the ministry. That wasn't the vision. We had no plans for the blog other than crowd control and crisis management, but something interesting happened. It began to make a deep impact.

My son and his story resonated deeply, and people became invested—fervently. The 400,000 unique impressions quickly grew to countless daily visits to the site as people all around the globe read about our journey and joined the prayer network. It was amazing to see that this little life, our tiny son who hadn't met anyone in person other than close family and his medical team, was making a significant impact on the wider world.

His early days had already taken on monumental meaning. He was the smallest unspeaking evangelist the world may have ever heard of. People's faith was growing. Many were finding renewal in their relationship with God. Some were even receiving the gift of salvation through my son's struggle.

I remember one day someone approached me at a bad time and told me that my son's story was shaping their faith and helping them to "get their 'stuff' together" (they didn't use the word "stuff"). While I can appreciate their candor and authenticity now, at the time, I complained to my mother.

"How dare they use my son's suffering and his story to get their 'stuff' together?"

It wasn't until the silent, lonely car ride home from the hospital that day that I heard clearly from the Lord on that matter.

"Really, John?" He asked. "Are you really tired of *your* son's suffering helping people get their 'stuff' together?"

Touché, God. You win. You always do.

I heard Him loud and clear. There I was dealing with my vast feelings of self-pity and insecurity, wondering if my life could ever recover any value or normalcy and if I'd ever be able to have an impact in ministry again. And at that moment, the grace of God filled my car and revealed how my little son's life was having a profound impact, silent as it was laying in that expansive incubator that should have been an intimate womb. My son's life was a living declaration, a testimony, a monument to the immeasurable measure of God's greatness, faithfulness, and power. A good God scripted his story, and in his fragility, my son was making a difference, without speaking a single word.

—

You matter. Your life matters. You are significant.

God was also extending an invitation to me. I had been striving, traveling, recording, speaking—all these ministry "things"—but I found myself sitting in the self-pity of my insecurity and a fear of insignificance. All the while, my son was doing little more than breathing. I cannot overemphasize the supernatural miracle of every one of his tiny, life-giving breaths, but that's all he was doing: just breathing, existing. However, as God had intended for him, he was living a message out loud to a watching world. His story, as it unfolded, was telling an even greater, more significant story.

And because of my son's story, I can say with confidence that God has also scripted *your* story. He knows each day of your life, the number of hairs on your head, and the sum total of every breath you will take. God created you on purpose, for purpose, because He wanted to.

You matter. Your life matters. *You* are significant.

As I said before, God intentionally designed you and your life and set you in the storyboard of time exactly when and where He wanted to. It's for such a time as this that you exist. Your life will represent something, and you have a significant story to tell! God has an incredible plan for your life, and you can live each day with this vision in view.

Your life can be monumental and lived with a fervent passion as a memorial to God's greatness, faithfulness, and power. It *is* possible! God is building a monument in His people, which includes *you*! And I hope to encourage that journey in you, starting right now—today.

Pray this prayer with me:

Jesus, I want nothing more than to honor You and live a significant life of purpose and impact. Help me over these next few chapters to get a clear vision for what You have created me for and are calling me to. I also pray that You will help me rest in who You created me to be, and not what the world's culture or even friends and family desire me to be. I want my life to become a monument to You, Your great Name, and Your power at work in and through me. Give me a sense of clarity, passion, and vision, I pray.

In Your Holy, mighty, powerful Name, Jesus. Amen.

01

TAKING THAT FIRST STEP

Psalm 29:18 (MSG)

If people can't see what God is doing,
they stumble all over themselves;

but when they attend to what He
reveals, they are most blessed.

Can You See It?

What is your vision for your life? What if I told you that God has an even greater vision for your life than you could ever dream, and He is inviting you to take a step of faith that could lead to a life you could never imagine for yourself? What if taking the first step, one act of faith, could create a monument of legacy? And what if it became clear that taking that first step would make the difference between never realizing your God-created purpose and living a profound, significant, monumental life?

I once heard a statement that stopped me in my tracks and made me ask God for greater clarity of vision: "Unless you see it before you see it, you'll never see it." (As much as I would love to give credit where credit is due, I'm not sure who originally made this powerful and profound statement.)

Think about it: Unless you have vision for something before you see it come to fruition, you will never see it come to fruition. This idea compels some critical questions: What do you find yourself dreaming about? Are you moving toward any goal or sense of purpose? Does something inside of you hunger for deeper meaning, reason, or impact?

—

God has a clear and powerful vision for your life.

Transcendence, or legacy, is something every human heart considers at some point. There comes a time when every single one of us begins to question our life out of a deep desire to ensure we are making an impact and leaving a mark. As the old maxim puts it, the life you choose to live will determine the legacy you leave behind. Intentionally or unintentionally, the way you choose to live your life, day by day, will have a consequential effect.

Here's the good news: God has a clear and powerful vision for your life. He always has! He created you on purpose and for purpose, so you can rest assured He has a plan, a path, and provision for everything you need to fulfill His good intentions for your life.

We don't have to bear the weight or pressure of performance in creating a vision for our life. We only need to embark on the journey God has called us to. Along the way, we will be called to take certain steps in certain seasons. There will be moments that require faith, when God invites us to move forward in obedience. There will be reaping from sowing. There will be valleys, mountains, deserts, and even potentially times of wilderness.

The challenge isn't how it all will end, but how we begin.

A God Vision

It was a random monument in the middle of a meadow that inspired me. It was years prior on a church planting trip in the northeast, on the campus of Williams College, when I came across this bronze and marble statue. The Haystack Monument, as it is known, commemorates the Haystack Prayer Meeting, which was held in August 1806 in Williamstown, Massachusetts.

At this prayer meeting, five Williams College students congregated to pray but also be commissioned by God with a massive vision. Samuel Mills, James Richards, Francis LeBaron Robbins, Harvey Loomis, and Byram Green gathered to discuss spiritual warfare, the people of Asia, and the theology of missionary service. At some point during the meeting, a thunderstorm interrupted them, and a heavy rain began to fall.

God is often like that. It's quite possible the rain was providential, as God was about to fall in a powerful way on this prayer meeting. I don't know what it is about students, but they are often the ones who usher in revival. This day would be no different. When the rain of God began to fall, many scattered, but these five men stayed, fixated on their purpose. They found shelter under a haystack and continued to meet and pray.

God met these men in that moment and placed a mandate in their hearts, which led them to continue gathering others to their cause. Two years after this moment of consecration, the group of five brought together even more students from Williams College. This is where they rented a sound system, built a stage, hired a minor Christian celebrity worship leader, set up the merch tent, and held a conference.

Just kidding. They didn't do any of that.

What they actually did was fervently pray, even more, with a group they called "The Brethren." They had developed, organized, and catalyzed this group, calling them to the mission of reaching those who were not Christ followers. By 1812, the American Board of Commissioners for Foreign Missions had sent its first missionaries to the non-Christian world in India. By 1817, it had launched the

Foreign Mission School, which was built in Cornwall, Connecticut. There, the group educated a total of one hundred students from different parts of the world, including India, Southwest Asia, and the Hawaiian Islands, as well as some Native Americans.

These five men may not be household names, but we have all been influenced by their devotion. The fruit of their faithfulness gave birth to what we now know as the foreign mission movement. Imagine that! How many people's lives have been eternally changed because of the obedience and faith of these few? And it all began with God's vision, accompanied by one small yet highly significant step. Simply by saying yes to attending that meeting, these men's lives became a monument with world-changing, significant meaning.

The Park Benches

As powerful and compelling as the story behind the Haystack Monument is, that is not what spoke the loudest to me that afternoon at Williams College. Of course, I was inspired reading the inscription and learning more about their world-changing story and ministry. And I was moved seeing the globe at the top of the pedestal and the message that had been memorialized in that place: "The field is the world."

It all began with God's vision, accompanied by one small yet highly significant step.

Something profoundly powerful and eternally necessary had catalyzed these men—something that, tragically, so many others willingly ignore. The gospel, and people knowing Jesus, was their priority, to the point that these men devoted the rest of their days to the call they received at that holy moment, in that holy place. What really struck me was not even the monument and its meaning, as powerful as that was. What got me, of all things, was the park benches that surrounded it.

As I stood still humbled and inspired by the monument and its meaning, God spoke to me regarding, of all things, the park benches. It was as if He whispered to me, "Are you willing to die to yourself and give your life as a monument to me, or will you settle for sitting on the sidelines as a spectator, watching others I call?"

That landed hard. It was like the rain of God was falling again in that place, and now God was asking me to join in His moving.

"Will you let me use your life to give it so much meaning that it becomes a memorial to my name? Are you willing to walk with me in faith, obedience, passion, and purpose, or will you watch other people walk in faith, obedience, passion, and purpose while waiting it out?"

Long ago, I had been irreparably changed by something Dr. Henry Blackaby suggested in his brilliant work *Experiencing God*: "Look where God is moving and join Him there."

When God Invites Us

What step is God inviting you to take for Him and *with* Him? You don't have to create or curate a vision for your life when the Creator already has one. His heart has been for you from the beginning. His vision for your life will be far greater than any idea, dream, or vision you can come up with for yourself, so you can trust Him.

You don't have to create or curate a vision for your life when the Creator already has one.

When God invites us into His vision, we can rest assured that His plans are undeniably amazing! Ephesians 3:20 in the New Living Translation puts it this way: *"Now all glory to God, who is able, through his mighty power at work within us, to accomplish infinitely more than we might ask or think."*

Whatever the vision or the faith step may be, the ultimate purpose of it all, including our life, is for the explicit glory of God. As the verse says, God, who is inviting you to step into His greatest intentions, can do surpassingly more than you or I could ever dream, create, curate, imagine, or ask. He is not only more than able but also more than willing, and He desires to accomplish His best work within you! He desires to accomplish His greatest plans and purposes—through your life!

The same verse of Scripture is beautifully interpreted by Eugene Peterson in his paraphrase called The Message. He writes, "God can do anything, you know—far more than you could ever imagine or guess or request in your wildest dreams! He does it not by pushing us around but by working within us, his Spirit deeply and gently within us."

—

You can only imagine what may come from your steps of obedience and faith, and it always starts the same way—with that first step.

I so love the way he expresses this momentous truth. God accomplishes amazing, supernatural things with us and through us, *not* by pushing us around but by working within us.

Begin to look where God is moving and simply take that first step to join Him there. You can only imagine what may come from your steps of obedience and faith, and it always starts the same way—with that first step. Remember, the challenge isn't how it all will end, but how we will begin.

The Great Invitation to Faith

Abram became no stranger to the process of hearing from God, counting the cost, and choosing to trust Him, beginning with that first significant step. His story is a riveting one. Imagine God interrupting your normal, seemingly satisfying life, showing up in your comfortable living room one day to invite you to take a step of faith and obedience.

While it may sound like a simple thing, the consequence of that step would require you to leave everything you've ever loved and known behind, to embrace the unknown based on very little information, except that you will become a blessing to the world.

We read Abram's story in Genesis 12 (NLT):

The LORD had said to Abram, "Leave your native country, your relatives, and your father's family, and go to the land that I will show you. I will make you into a great nation. I will bless you and make you famous, and you will be a blessing to others. I will bless those who bless you and curse those who treat you with contempt. All the families on earth will be blessed through you."

I don't personally believe that Haran was supposed to be Abram's home, but through a series of events, it was all Abram had ever really known. Now, God was telling him, "If you take this step, Abram, I'll bless you. I'll introduce you to a world you could never imagine. I'll do things in and through your life that will register on the Richter scale. However, it will require you to leave behind your comfortable life. Leave behind the life you've built here. Leave behind your inheritance. I know you're seventy-five years old, Abram, and I know I'm not telling you any specific latitude or longitude for your destination. But I am telling you that in order to embrace this life of destiny and legacy, you will have to leave. Take the step, follow me, and I will bless you and make your name great."

God has a way of exalting those who exalt Him. He doesn't necessarily make them famous in the way our culture craves fame and fortune, but when God highlights someone, His intention is to use their life in great measure for great meaning.

When God highlights someone, His intention is to use their life in great measure for great meaning.

God told Abram the reward for his faith and obedience would be a great name, blessing, affluence, influence, and legacy. God would make his name great, God would bless him, and God would use his life to bless others. His promise to Abram was not just to bless a few, but that He would use Abram's life to bless *every family on the earth*!

Wow, talk about a vision. Talk about a potent promise—but still, a promise that would come with a price. It would potentially cost Abram everything he knew and held close. Can you imagine what he must have felt when taking that first step?

The Requirements of the RSVP

If we are to answer the call of God and take that step of faith with Him to walk into a monumental life, it will come at a price. God's dream for our life could cost us everything we've held dear. In Luke 9:23 (ESV), Jesus declared, "If anyone would come after me, let him deny himself and take up his cross daily and follow me."

—

Choosing to live a monumental life is choosing to live a sacrificial life.

This means choosing to live a monumental life is choosing to live a sacrificial life. We can't hear the words from God, "I'll bless you" and believe that means blessing by our own cultural definitions. God's blessing can look many ways, but rarely is it a worldly way.

Abram has a choice: On the one hand, he could continue to live in the comfort of his country and the familiarity of his family and enjoy his days. Eventually, he would receive the inheritance of his relatives and all that his father had acquired. That sounds like a pretty decent gig. On the other hand, the Creator of the universe was inviting Abram to follow Him into the unknown, guaranteeing him a life like he'd never known.

What Abram knew was most likely pretty satisfying and would contribute to a fairly satisfying legacy, but the risk was having to settle for so much less. What life would he really want to live, and what legacy would he really want to leave in his wake? Choosing to take this step with God could be the difference between never realizing his God-created purpose and potential or living a profound and significant monumental life—a life full of what God calls "blessing."

A monument of land that had been promised to God's people stands today to preserve not only the promise of God to Abraham and his offspring, but also to preserve the memory of the goodness and faithfulness of God to His own.

What If

What about those five Williams College students? What if they had skipped out on the fateful meeting that day? What if they had operated like we normally operate in our culture, receiving the invitation to spiritual significance but waiting to see if anything better would come along? What if they had run from the rain instead of seeking the shelter at the nearest haystack, determined to pray? In that moment, I believe God put revival in their hearts and a passion to reach the world with the gospel. No counteroffer competing for their attention and allegiance, and no moment of bad weather, could stop them from taking that step of faith.

A monument stands today to preserve not only the providence and power of God's calling, anointing, and ability, but also to preserve the memory of what God whispered to those men that day, a blessing that would change the world.

What if I told you that one small step, which may seem insignificant in your eyes, could be the world-altering catalyst? The decisions you make and the way you live your life, whether intentionally or unintentionally, will leave a mark in some way. You will have an impact on many people. Your life is significant because you were created for significance by a supernatural and significant God. God is writing a greater story through your life, and it is a story of legacy.

—

The decisions you make and the way you live your life, whether intentionally or unintentionally, will leave a mark in some way.

What is God's vision for your life? If you don't begin to see it in faith before you see it to fruition, sadly you'll never see it at all, and that would be a great tragedy. Abram had to see in faith that God was worth following. Now, it's your turn. Remember, He isn't a bully. He won't push you around, but He'll knock and wait for you to open the door. He wants to work in and through your life for His glory and for your good. He's writing a story, here and now. Will you answer Him? Will you take that first step?

Your Part in the Story

We all have a story to tell since we are all part of God's story, but we also have an enemy who wants to steal, kill, and destroy—who desires to keep us from God's calling and destiny. The enemy is sly, cunning, and wildly deviant in his desire for your destruction. Not only will he do all he can to derail and discourage you, his ultimate goal is actually to destroy you before you begin to step into God's destiny for your life. He'll use anything within reach, especially things like your past failures, insecurities, traumas, and fears. He'll work to sift and tempt you, all the while taunting you. The last thing he wants is for you to live your life as a memorial to the goodness and faithfulness of God.

It is important that we recognize, even as the story of our life is being scripted, that there are powers working against us, trying to unravel our life before our greatest purpose is revealed. I'm sure Abram had his own struggles. I know I've had mine, and I'm sure you too will face a struggle even before you get to chapter 2. The struggle will take the form of questions like these: *But God, who am I? Why would You call me to anything, let alone call my name at all? God, don't You know what I've done? You may be able, but I'm completely incapable. I'm not qualified. In fact, I've made decisions and done things that disqualify me. I want what You have for me, but I'm scared I'll fail, and I don't know if I can really trust You.*

Can I be the first to say welcome to the club? No doubt, Abraham dealt with the same thoughts, fears, and emotions, and I fight them as well. As a charter lifetime member of the "I'm not qualified for such a task" club, I open my arms wide to you.

In fact, in the next few chapters, we'll tackle these very doubts to reveal just how weak and feckless the enemy's tactics are in comparison to God's truth. My prayer and greatest desire in writing this book is to encourage and challenge you so that you begin to see what God is doing and then start moving into the monumental destiny He planned for your life.

Are you ready to take whatever step God is inviting you to take?

Pray this prayer with me:

Father, would you bring stillness to any chaos that may surround me and silence to any created voice speaking, that I may only hear from the voice of You, my Creator? Tune my heart to hear Your whisper and my eyes to see Your ways. Give me a clear vision for where You are moving in my life and prepare me for the monumental life You are calling me to live.

I pray in Your mighty name, Jesus. Amen.

02

OBSTACLES TO OBEDIENCE

Isaiah 56:5 (NLT)

I will give them—within the walls of my house—a memorial and a name

far greater than sons and daughters could give. For the name I give them

is an everlasting one. It will never disappear!

Mountains, Walls, Giants

A near-debilitating level of insecurity already ran in my bloodstream by the time I was fifteen years old. I can't exactly diagnose why, other than that age is inherently awkward for a teenage male, but I found myself gripped by it. It was, after all, the "Z Cavaricci" years, to date myself. Need I say more? (Feel free to Google that little blessing. Once you hit the right website, don't be surprised if your computer suddenly begins to supernaturally emit the aroma of Drakkar Noir.)

I can't say why I was so committed to that struggle bus. It could have been from living through the lens of comparison, or it could have been because I was *the last Gen X kid* in Huntsville, Texas, to get that famous pair of Kaepa shoes with those little interchangeable triangles. It also probably didn't help that I didn't own a pair of parachute pants at the very moment they were trending, which would have surely solidified my social standing. I was also late to the Swatch watch game and equally late to the Members Only jacket club. So yeah, not having any drip like that in those days probably didn't help, but I digress.

In all seriousness, I'm sure that's not what really caused such big feelings of alienation and anxiety. Looking back now, I yearn for the simplicity of that age—but not its emotional fragility. Back then, the slightest sense of rejection would send me into a swift emotional spiral. At my age now, I have the luxury of hindsight as well as the ability to see clearly just how the enemy uses even the smallest of our emotions to keep us contained.

Make no mistake: We have an enemy, the devil, who is an accusing and vile liar. He will do anything he can to rob you of everything that God has in store for you. One of his favorite tactics to lock us up is through voicing his curses to our vulnerabilities. He will do everything he can to derail our destiny by placing obstacles in our path to challenge our obedience. He loves nothing more than to see a child of God, who has been rescued and redeemed by God, choose to live like they're an orphan of God. We can even read Scriptures like Ephesians 1:5 (ESV), where Paul gives this bold prophetic declaration over us: "He has predestined us for adoption to Himself as sons through Jesus Christ, according to the purpose of His will"—and still believe the lies of the enemy which are designed to keep us stuck in uncertainty.

A Monumental Moment

I found myself at a student camp in Albuquerque that summer (no Z Cavariccis in my luggage, for those wondering), surrounded by nine hundred of my closest friends (not really). It was a crowded room, but somehow I still found a way to feel incredibly alone. It wasn't that I didn't have a personality, and it wasn't that I couldn't be mischievous and get a laugh out of whatever small audience I might find. At least if people were laughing with me, they weren't pointing at me.

In reality, I was a fairly shy, functionally introverted, skateboarding drummer. Those were the two things I cared about in life: skateboarding (surely I was going to be the next Tony Hawk) and drumming (because of Alex Van Halen, hello?!). However, it was at that student camp that, for the first time, I encountered the true glory of God for myself. I had grown up in church and attended countless services. I had a healthy belief in God, but it was sort of like believing in Santa Claus to me, except for real. That night, worship was being led by a guy named—I kid you not—Jimmy Jimmerson. Yes, that was his real name as far as I know. I'm sure Mr. Jimmerson was an outstanding guy, but I couldn't say I was particularly into his music, despite being an aspiring musician myself.

I don't remember anything special happening the night the Spirit of God decided to rest upon that room and breathe upon me. It just happened. Suddenly, I felt His breath upon my life. The weight of His glory was palpable enough to wreck me in such a way that I not only gave Him my full surrender but also committed the totality of my life to Him for ministry.

It was a monumental moment in my life. I didn't yet fully know what it meant. At fifteen, it didn't really make sense, but I knew that for the first time, I had encountered the vast goodness of God—and I couldn't walk away the same. I am convinced that God spoke to me and called me to something involving music and students.

It didn't make a lot of sense at the time, but I trusted that God was speaking to me, calling me, and inviting me down a path that deserved my yes, even if I didn't fully understand it.

"But God, I *am* a student," I protested.

Like I said, it didn't make a lot of sense at the time, but I trusted that God was speaking to me, calling me, and inviting me down a path that deserved my yes, even if I didn't fully understand it. As with Abraham's call, there was no destination given, only a whispered invitation to destiny. Had God given me a blueprint of the journey, I'm not sure what I would have done, but there I was at the altar giving God my yes.

Next step: the little room.

The Little Room

I had seen, and been in, the little room before. When God is moving in a mighty way, in order to allow for a meaningful conversation, pastors would often direct people at the altar to move to an outside room where they could fully process what God was doing. I remember being ushered into a little room at nine years old after following my big sister down the aisle to meet a pastor one Sunday, when God had landed on her life. I admired my big sis, so I wouldn't let her go alone. I went with her, received my "Welcome to the Family" new believer's book, and was assigned to the deacon of the week for "accountability."

—

God doesn't only call the qualified. God qualifies those He calls.

That didn't last long, sad to say—but now, at camp, with God moving, it was totally different and incredibly real to me. I found myself taken into the camp's version of "the little room," but thankfully, the leaders paired me with one of the young adult sponsors from our church, whom I looked up to.

"Alex, I don't understand, and I don't know what to do," I remember saying. "I'm nowhere qualified to do 'ministry,' and after all, students? I mean, heck, I'm still a student myself. And music? All I do is play the drums. How can God use that, and how can God use me? I'm just a shy, skateboarding drummer."

I will *never* forget what Alex said to me that day, and I want to say it to you because you may feel some of the same things I felt way back then. It's also possible that you too have dealt with deep feelings of insecurity when it comes to imagining a God-breathed call upon your life. Most people don't feel like they have anything to offer, and this is exactly what our enemy wants. He wants to prevent us from even considering the potential of having a life of eternal impact. The devil would rather render us idle on the sidelines than let us understand our identity in Christ and be active on the frontlines. So if you are struggling with insecurity, this is for you as much as it was for me.

Alex looked me dead in the eye and said, "John, I want you to really hear what I'm about to tell you. God doesn't only call the qualified. God qualifies those He calls."

Alex's Word Is Also for You

Now, maybe you've heard that little axiom before, but let me tell you, even thirty-five years later, that statement means more to me than ever.

God doesn't only call the qualified. God qualifies those He calls.

I want you to understand the gravity of that statement. What can we take from it? Here are a few truths:

- God doesn't only pick the popular, athletic kids for His celestial kickball team.
- It's not who we are, what we can do, what we have to offer, or anything of our own agency that qualifies us.
- It's God and God alone who chooses, and it's God and God alone who qualifies.

Jesus modeled this fact for us. When choosing His disciples, He didn't go find all the elite Jewish kids of proper pedigree from the "Religious Preparatory Academy of the Torah." Jesus didn't even choose from the righteous privileged. He went and gathered a band of young, teenage misfits, most likely already overlooked and rejected by all the other rabbis, and He called them and placed a mantle upon their lives that would leave behind a monumental legacy.

Today, *we* are part of their legacy. Isn't it good to know that Jesus loves misfits? Truth be told, that is *the only* explanation for my being in ministry, and I'm okay with that. I'm completely comfortable aligning myself with the ragamuffin gang of misfits who just want to continue to encounter and follow Jesus and nothing else. It's by following close in the dust of the rabbi Jesus that we find the monumental life He has prepared for us.

More Barriers to Belief

Let's go back to our friend Abram. He chose to obey God, take the first step, and leave Haran as the Lord had instructed. The Scripture says he was seventy-five years old when he took that first step of radical obedience and faith. Don't think for one moment that his age wasn't a consideration to him. Don't think for one moment he didn't question his qualification.

The Bible makes it clear as day in Genesis 12:4. I can only imagine Abram thinking, *But God, I'm seventy-five years old! What business do I have starting this "choose your own adventure" plot twist now?*

While his age probably didn't help with feelings of qualification for God's calling, his situation is great news for us. Let Abram's story encourage you that if there is still breath in your lungs, there are still things God has for you to do!

Obviously, God concerns Himself more with our obedience to His assignments than the potential obstacle of age. When God calls your name, you'd better believe that your best days aren't behind you. You may have already lived what you would describe as the blessings of a thousand lives, but God may yet have another assignment for you that will demand a step of faith and obedience. And that next assignment could be far more fulfilling than you ever dreamed.

—

There's always blessing on the other side of obedience—so don't stop looking for where God is moving.

The point is, there's always blessing on the other side of obedience—so don't stop looking for where God is moving, and don't allow yourself to sit down and settle. Age is simply a number, never a disqualifier. Even at seventy-five, Abram's monumental life was really just beginning.

Eventually, his journey brought him through the land, as Scripture says, as far as Shechem. Shechem would have been about 550 miles from Abram's home of Haran, so at this point, he was deeply committed. It was at Shechem that he set up camp, and that's when we see it: Scripture says in Genesis 12:6 (NLT), "At that time, the area was inhabited by Canaanites."

I wonder if Abram wondered, *Wait. Was it God's intention to lead me to this inhabited place?* God then showed up to give Abram a little pep talk, telling him that He intended to give that very land to his descendants. God was giving him a vision for what *could be*, but Abram had to be willing to *look past what was.*

Don't miss this.

The very land that was currently inhabited by others would become part of Abram's legacy. So, regardless of what Abram could (or couldn't) see, he built an altar at that very place and dedicated it to the Lord, who, Scripture says, "had appeared to him" there. In faith, Abram built a monument, both to memorialize God's provision and to remind future generations of God's promise.

God Always Provides for His Purposes

I'm sure this was a moment of relief and encouragement for Abram, so let it encourage you too. When God calls you to something that requires great faith, He will provide everything necessary to see His promises come to fruition. You may look up and see your land currently inhabited, but when God speaks, you can put a stake in the ground, build a monument, and worship, because God will move on your behalf!

It's God who led Abram there and it'll be God who leads you to your Shechem. Remember, Shechem was just one stop on the path of God's promise, so it didn't end there. As Abram continued on, a severe famine drove him and his family to Egypt, where he was forced to live as an unwelcome foreigner. If not for his beautiful wife, surely he would have been killed.

The story is nothing short of a soap opera, but the point I want to make is no one promises the road to a monumental life will be an easy one. Your first step of faith won't be the only step of faith required. In fact, I'd say every step you take will demand a decent amount of faith and resolve. And with every step taken, there will be more opportunities to question your qualifications as well as to question God's call. Inhabitants will appear. Famines will come. Your faith, fortitude, leadership, and legacy will be tested and called into question—but keep going, because God is faithful.

Your faith, fortitude, leadership, and legacy will be tested and called into question—but keep going, because God is faithful. Just when you feel there is no way, God will make a way.

Just when you feel there is no way, God will make a way. After all, to once again quote Eugene Peterson in his paraphrase of 1 Thessalonians 5:24, "The One who called you is completely dependable. If He said it, He'll do it!"

God's Assignments & the Enemy's Accusations (Another Goliath)

Another of the enemy's tactics to try to keep us from the monumental life God is calling us to live is to remind us of our past mistakes. He speaks the language of accusation and condemnation. His taunting and tormenting can quickly derail you and cause deep, dark feelings of disqualification.

It's ironic how God can forgive and choose not to remember our past sin and mistakes, but oh, how we struggle to forgive ourselves. God speaks mercy over our lives, but the enemy spits misery—and for whatever reason, his voice seems to be amplified even louder. King David is a great example of this dynamic. The man we know as one who pursued the very heart of God was also the man who pursued the lull of lust. He found himself in the wrong place at the wrong time doing the wrong things. Let this be a lesson to us on our journey:

Right Place + Right Time = Right Things
Wrong Place + Wrong Time = Wrong Things

We read his story in 2 Samuel 11. King David should have gone to battle with his troops, but instead, he stayed home in bed. God had given him the privilege of being king, but he arose from the lazy slumber of a midday nap, only to stroll on his rooftop and peer down on the wife of one of his soldiers, who happened to be bathing. Promiscuously intrigued, the king inquired who this woman was.

"That's Bathsheba, the daughter of Eliam and the wife of Uriah," he was told.

Don't let that statement slip by, because it is everything you need to know regarding David's state of mind. When we willingly shelve our leadership for laziness, we shouldn't be surprised to find ourselves with an all-too-easy propensity toward sin.

The woman David was inquiring about was someone's daughter and someone's wife. The rest of the sordid, salacious story is that he sent for her, slept with her, and impregnated her. If that wasn't enough, he then tried to cover up his depraved deed by having her husband brought home from war to rest and be with his wife. When that plan backfired, due to Uriah's fidelity to his king and his brothers at battle, David concocted a plan to put Uriah on the frontline and let nature take its course.

—

When we willingly shelve our leadership for laziness, we shouldn't be surprised to find ourselves with an all-too-easy propensity toward sin.

So here's the story of a man God had called to be a monumental king, but he committed adultery and murder. Were there consequences for his callousness and carnality? Yes, absolutely. His sin actually cost him greatly. However, did God disqualify David? No, not necessarily. David wasn't exactly the point of the story, but he was definitely an important part. David's kingship was intended to be a prophetic monument pointing to someone greater who was to come: the King of Kings, Jesus, who would come through the lineage of King David to defeat sin once and for all. Though King David dealt with significant fallout from his own epic failures, God's goodness was still memorialized and displayed through David's life and story.

Please don't hear my benevolent way of describing David's downfall in any way as an endorsement of his actions. While God forgave David and didn't remove him from his assignment, David's actions invited some severe consequences that should serve as a warning to us all. David lost his child to death, as well as his sense of peace. His actions brought strife to his kingdom.

However, no matter what we do, God is ultimately the one we must answer to. With that said, here's something else to note.

David's brokenness over his blatant disregard of God and God's people led him to receive undeserved mercy and grace. God wasn't done with David, and God isn't done with you. No matter what you may have done, no matter what your grievous sin may have been, if God is the one who calls and qualifies then God is the one who gets to call for disqualification.

—

Yes, our capacity for disobedience is great, but praise God that His capacity for grace is greater! The undeserved grace of God is unbound, relentless, and immeasurable.

Has someone's disobedience to God caused them to be disqualified by God? I'd refer you to King Saul's story, Cain's story, Esau's story, even King Solomon's story to a degree—so yes, God has disqualified people and removed their assignments and blessings. It's important for us to know *why* God would do this. When God chooses to disqualify someone and remove their assignment, sometimes, it's out of justice and His faithfulness. Sometimes, it's our abdication of our assignment and blessing that calls for God's disqualification.

God will get His desire, one way or another. With that said, please know that God continually gives us opportunity after opportunity to repent and be restored. That is simply who He is. There is nothing that God can't resurrect, restore, or redeem! It's also important to know that God does not disqualify people for the purpose of punishment or condemnation. Remember, Jesus didn't come to condemn us, but to save us! He didn't condemn the woman caught in adultery, though He did tell her to go and sin no more.

Yes, our capacity for disobedience is great, but praise God that His capacity for grace is greater! The undeserved grace of God is unbound, relentless, and immeasurable. I mean, consider Judas. There's a guy we assume should have been, and was, disqualified, but as Ephesians 2:4 says, ... "*but God!*" Now before you come at me, please remember Jesus not only implored Judas, giving him multiple opportunities to do the right thing, but He even washed Judas's feet and allowed Judas at His table. Jesus continually spoke graciously to Judas, even to the end. It wasn't Jesus's idea for Judas to hang himself; it was the voice of the accusing, condemning liar that led Judas to end his life.

The Right Voice

We need to be very careful regarding which voice we choose to listen to. God's voice is quite discernable when considering His character. God's language is that of love and grace, while the enemy speaks the language of hatred and condemnation. God will never speak to you in a way that would cause shame. When it comes to Jesus, mercy triumphs over judgment in every way, so allow His mercy to triumph over the judgment of the world, over the condemning words of the enemy, and over the judgment you place upon your own past mistakes.

Also consider the woman at the well in John 4. Here was a woman who was going daily to a public well, often at a different time than the rest of the other women in order to avoid judgment and rejection. Every day, she would go to satisfy her thirst, and then *that* day came. Doing what she habitually did, she approached Jacob's well to find a Jewish rabbi named Jesus hanging out there, as if waiting for her. I mean, no one else was around. Why in the world would a Jewish rabbi be at that place? Why would a Jewish man, who would culturally have nothing to do with a mixed-up, religiously idolatrous Samaritan woman—especially a known promiscuous woman—be in Samaria at all?

The conversation that followed was His plan the whole time, for the explicit purpose of inviting her to transformation.

"Go and get your husband," Jesus said.

"I don't have a husband," she replied.

"You're right about that. You've had five husbands and the one you are with now isn't even your husband."

This led to a bit of religious debate, but upon Jesus revealing His true identity to this woman, she ended up leaving that place (along with her water jars, which was the reason she was there in the first place) to run back into town and tell everyone what had happened to her. In a way that only Jesus could, He offered her mercy, and it was in this moment that she traded her shame for salvation.

She ran back home declaring all that had happened, and she ended up catalyzing a revival in her city. Many believed in Jesus because of her story. And to think, she woke up that day the same way she woke up every morning, doing the same mundane things she did in the same way. However, that day, everything changed because she encountered Jesus. Her life, once marked by sin and shame, was now a memorial to the goodness of God. Her transformation was a miracle that became a monument, as God took her story and gave her His.

Imagine the tragic consequences if she had chosen to ignore the voice of Jesus for the voices of others!

In Isaiah 56, the Lord speaks about eunuchs. Biblically, a eunuch was a man who had been castrated, rendered ineffectual and unable to bear children, which culturally meant he had no blessing or true legacy. In a time and place where everything hinged upon the blessing of children, lineage, and legacy, imagine the emotional turmoil and anguish eunuchs experienced.

With that thought in mind, please hear me: You may feel completely ineffectual. You may feel like you'll never know blessing, that someone like you could never leave a lasting lineage or legacy. However, the mercy of God speaks to those who feel ineffectual and who feel like they have no ability to live a life of blessing or legacy. Beginning in verse 3 of Isaiah 56 (NLT), God says:

Don't let the eunuchs say, "I'm a dried-up tree with no children and no future." For this is what the LORD says: I will bless those eunuchs who keep my Sabbath days holy and who choose to do what pleases me and commit their lives to me. I will give them—within the walls of my house— a memorial and a name far greater than sons and daughters could give. For the name I give them is an everlasting one. It will never disappear!

What does this mean to us? In a broader sense, I believe God is telling us not to listen to the accusations, labels, and identities that the culture may put upon us. When the enemy, the culture, or anyone in the world tries to make us feel insignificant, disqualified, or unqualified in any way, God says otherwise.

For those who commit their ways to Him, God has a place of priority. He has a legacy for them that's greater than anything even children could ever provide. Their lives will become a memorial of God's favor and will be a monument of God's faithfulness. The calling of God is everlasting! What a beautiful and profound truth that no one can take away from us.

We can't allow the enemy, the culture of this world, or anyone to define our value, our worth, our ability, our potential, our significance, or our qualification. God and God alone is our validation, and His word over us is blessing. He calls us, and He qualifies us.

Pray this prayer with me:

Father, would you bring stillness to any chaos surrounding me and silence to any created voice speaking, that I may only hear from the voice of You, my Creator? Help me to believe that You are my validation and that only You are able to bring qualification. In this, reveal to me Your heart for me.

I pray this in Your mighty name, Jesus. Amen.

03

THE ENEMY OF FAITH & FULFILLMENT

> Isaiah 41:13 (NLT)
> For I hold you by your right hand—I, the LORD your God.
> And I say to you, "Don't be afraid. I am here to help you."

The Fear Monster

If insecurity is the libelous thief of an impactful life, then fear is the enemy of faith and fulfillment. Fear has the ability to incapacitate you and keep you from taking that leap of faith toward a monumental life. I wish I could say I mastered this long ago, but the truth is it's taken me years to get to the place I'm in.

Galatians 2:20 (NASB) has been a life verse to me for the last twenty-seven years, sometimes a lifeline. Paul says: "I have been crucified with Christ, and it is no longer I who live, but Christ lives in me; and the life which I now live in the flesh I live by faith in the Son of God, who loved me and gave Himself up for me."

Please know, when I say, "life verse," I didn't choose it—it chose me. One could call it the "Calvinist verse" that jumped off the page and grabbed me by the throat. I *did not* want to embrace it. Why? I had a sober, clear sense that Paul's words "I've been crucified with Christ" were the crux of true Christianity in practice. Those words are a mirror that ruthlessly and relentlessly examines my heart and motives daily.

Fear is a lying, mocking monster.

Jesus gave prescriptive words when He invited people to follow Him by dying to self, taking up your cross, and following in His steps. Paul's words describe putting Jesus's teaching into action. *Die to self.*

Dietrich Bonhoeffer had it right when he said, "When Christ calls a man, He bids him to come and die." In other words, if we are to follow Jesus truly, it's not going to be an easy path but one that demands the violent and willing crushing of your own will. It requires a radical transformation accompanied by a readiness to relinquish your own desires, ambitions, dreams, insecurities, and fears.

Fear? Ugh.

Keeping It Real

I'm choosing to be vulnerable here. Fear has been the elephant in the room with me and the giant standing in my path for some time now. Fear is a lying, mocking monster. Whether it be fear of failure, fear of rejection, or fear of comparison, I am guilty of all of it. I can't say how many years fear has kept me on the sidelines instead of at bat. It's as if I've found myself content in the dugout but never at the plate.

Forgive the baseball analogy if it's not your thing. Let me put it this way: Fear is the enemy's way of keeping us rendered feckless. It's fear that keeps many of us stuck, unable to reach our purpose and potential. The devil is so cunning. He knows that if he can hold us captive in the grip of fear, he will incapacitate us and keep us from God's promises. He's also a deviant who is perfectly okay with us claiming Christ as long as it doesn't involve actually living in the identity and power Christ died to offer us.

This is his aim for our lives: to steal from us, rob us of joy and blessing, and destroy our destiny before we can dive into it. As John 10:10 declares, the devil would love nothing more than to kill us. The enemy wants us removed from the equation, along with our God-given dreams and desires, through his vice grip of fear. Something I've been learning for years is that the fear of failure is the antithesis of walking in faith. I've had plenty of experience wrestling various Goliaths of fear, but now I know that in order to step into the fullness of what God has prepared for us, in order to live a monumental life, we must slay the giant of our fear. Again, the enemy of faith and fulfillment is fear.

—

If the devil can hold us captive in the grip of fear, he will incapcitate us and keep us from God's promises.

We Aren't Alone

Many great men and women in the Bible heard God whisper an invitation and chose to take a bold step of faith that would impact the world in some way.

"Noah, I want you to build a big boat."

"Why? Oh, to save the world from evil. Got it."

—

The enemy of faith and fulfillment is fear.

"Joshua and Caleb, I want you to take ten spies and explore the promised land. Report back what you find."

Joshua and Caleb came back ready, but the other spies were gripped by fear of the giants they saw there. "Forget the land of fruition, fulfillment, and promise. There are giants who are too strong for us," they said. Even though God would have been on their side, they let fear hinder them from receiving His promise.

Sadly, the world is full of "spies" who are all too willing to focus only on what is right in front of them. All too often, faith is sacrificed on the altar of fear, which comes with great consequences. Tragically, today there are far too many who are quick to give a negative report and settle for thinking the assignment—and God's potential blessing—isn't worth the battle.

What if Abraham had decided the invitation into the unknown was too great to justify the loss of what he already knew? That may have been the end of his story. God probably would have moved on from Abraham to find someone else who wouldn't allow fear to triumph over faith. After all, it is God who does the inviting, so we can be confident that we are in good hands.

—

All too often, faith is sacrificed on the altar of fear.

Moses is another great case study regarding fear. Of course, there is an important difference between the fear of God, which we call reverence, and simply fear. Moses displayed both of these in the account of his supernatural call from God to live a monumental life.

This plays out in the first six verses of Exodus 3 (NLT):

One day, Moses was tending the flock of his father-in-law, Jethro, the priest of Midian. He led the flock far into the wilderness and came to Sinai, the mountain of God. There, the angel of the Lord appeared to him in a blazing fire from the middle of a bush. Moses stared in amazement. Though the bush was engulfed in flames, it didn't burn up. "This is amazing," Moses said to himself. "Why isn't that bush burning up? I must go see it."

I love this imagery. It reminds me of something John Wesley supposedly said: "Get on fire for God, and people will come to watch you burn." Moses sees a bush on fire yet not consumed. He finds himself enamored with such a supernatural sight, and he is compelled to draw closer to get a better look:

When the Lord saw Moses coming to take a closer look, God called to him from the middle of the bush, "Moses! Moses!"

[It's when we draw close that we begin to hear God's whisper grow louder.]

"Moses! Moses!"

"Here I am!" Moses replied [perhaps reluctantly].

"Do not come any closer," the Lord warned. "Take off your sandals, for you are standing on holy ground. I am the God of your father—the God of Abraham, the God of Isaac, and the God of Jacob." When Moses heard this, he covered his face because he was afraid to look at God.

Redefining Fear

We see Moses draw close to such a wondrous sight, only to become overwhelmed by God's voice and realize that this encounter is much more than he anticipated. Moses assumes an appropriate posture before the holiness of God, something our current generations could take a cue from. The nearness of God brings with it new levels of holiness, so you should posture yourself accordingly. Even the ground is holy where God is, so Moses adjusts his wonder to reverence or, more accurately, holy fear.

It's when we draw close that we begin to hear God's whisper grow louder.

This is a great case study for us in redefining fear. Our God is an awesome God, and our English language doesn't do justice when trying to define what "awesome" truly means. Moses is encountering something so otherworldly, something so completely supernatural, that he just can't contain himself.

And check this out: Though God is the one who invites Moses to draw closer, the holiness of God causes Moses to begin cowering and covering his face because of his fear of the potential of seeing God.

In this place, the Lord continues His conversation with Moses and offers him a call to destiny. The fruit of this call will not only redefine his fear but also yield a life that memorializes the greatness and goodness of God:

Then the Lord told him, "I have certainly seen the oppression of my people in Egypt. I have heard their cries of distress because of their harsh slave drivers. Yes, I am aware of their suffering. So I have come down to rescue them from the power of the Egyptians and lead them out of Egypt into their own fertile and spacious land. It is a land flowing with milk and honey—the land where the Canaanites, Hittites, Amorites, Perizzites, Hivites, and Jebusites now live. Look! The cry of the people of Israel has reached me, and I have seen how harshly the Egyptians abuse them. Now go, for I am sending you to Pharaoh. You must lead my people Israel out of Egypt."

—

We tend to give so much power to so many lesser things, which keeps us trapped in fear, unable to live our calling.

God's call to His people is usually about the rescue, restoration, and redemption of people. A monumental life is not focused on how many followers you attain, how much status you achieve, or how much money you accumulate—rather, it's a life lived to the glory of God, on the mission of rescue, restoration, and redemption of all things back to the Father. Yet we learn "Moses protested to God, '*Who am I to appear before Pharaoh? Who am I to lead the people of Israel out of Egypt?*'"

Who Am I?

This is a typical response, and understandably so. "Who am I, God?" "Are you speaking to me?" "Why me, Lord? You do know who I am... right?"

If I am honest, I completely understand Moses and his angst.

"Who am I, Lord, that You would choose me for such a task?"

"Who am I, God—I'm not qualified, I'm unqualified, I'm disqualified, I'm afraid."

"What will people say or think when I speak on *Your* behalf?"

"I'm nobody, God, nobody from nowhere. What do I have to offer? Why would anyone choose to listen to me or, worse yet, follow me?"

—

God will never call us to a life where He is unnecessary!

At this point in the story, God is about to send Moses as His chosen leader into not only a power structure but *the* power structure of the day. Regardless of God's call upon our lives, we tend to give so much power to so many lesser things, which keeps us trapped in fear, unable to live our calling. We tend to forget that there is no power structure greater than the power of our God, who is the one calling us, equipping us, empowering us, for us, and behind us. I've been guilty of it and understand this mental paradox. However, no matter how many times we allow ourselves to bow to the opinions of others, notice what God says to Moses: *"I will be with you."*

That should be enough, right? God promised Moses He would be with him, and we must know that the God who is, who was, and who is to come—that same God promises to be with *us*, as well. There is no calling or assignment He has for us that He expects us to handle on our own. In fact, I submit to you that God will never call us to a life where He is unnecessary! For every mission and mandate He calls us to, His presence will be mission critical.

Fear of failure is real, but so is FOMO (fear of missing out). I'd rather fail a million times while walking in faith and obedience to God en route to a monumental life than live a safe, ordinary, mundane life.

Another Giant to Confront

The fear of rejection is another giant the enemy loves to put in the path of purpose and promise. I say it's painful because the fear of rejection and abandonment has been a massive giant in my life for far too long. People come and go, sometimes all too easily. I've lost count of how many relationships I've poured my all into, only to find out they weren't what I thought they were or wanted them to be.

Rejection is incredibly painful, and if we allow it, the enemy will use it to debilitate us and keep us from God's destiny for our lives. We must be careful not to blame God for the pain caused by people abandoning us. People will come and go, but God will always remain.

There may be times when God has to purge relationships from our lives to drive us deeper into our relationship with Him. Though painful, there's usually a purpose in it. I once heard it said that "loyalty is a vain substitute for calling." It's tragic to think of how many people choose loyalty over legacy, even at the cost of living stuck and settled.

There's an adage that says, "Hold vision tightly and people lightly." While that may sound romantic, it's hard to put into practice. I *so* wish I could swallow that bitter pill. I've had a long line of leavers due to my calling, more than I care to recall, and that has been one of the toughest repercussions of this road God has me on. They say leadership is loneliness, but man, that's tough.

—

We must be careful not to blame God for the pain caused by people abandoning us.

Here's something we need to remember: When God calls you to a monumental life, that call doesn't necessarily extend to everyone around you. Remember, the Haystack Monument focused on five individuals, five guys who chose the radical road, despite the storm. It's not that others weren't involved, or that others didn't come and go, but God chooses the people He does, at His will, for what He desires. So, what did God do to address Moses's fears?

I mean, Moses had some *real* reservations about God's calling. He did not think people would believe him, or listen to him, or follow him—which is totally understandable. So, God encouraged him by saying He'd give him a sign:

"And this is your sign that I am the one who has sent you: When you have brought the people out of Egypt, you will worship God at this very mountain."

But Moses protested, "If I go to the people of Israel and tell them, 'The God of your ancestors has sent me to you,' they will ask me, 'What is his name?' Then what should I tell them?"

When God is on our side, there is no reason or room for fear.

God replied to Moses, "I am who I am. Say this to the people of Israel:

I Am has sent me to you."

In other words, Moses, tell them when they question you, *if* they question you, that the I AM—the one who *is* everything that they'd ever need, want, hope for, long for, or call upon—that is who sent you. "I AM" is the one who is also sending you, assigning you, and calling you to this life. You can rest and be reassured that no matter the power structures or the people God is calling you to, His calling is always about the rescue, restoration, and redemption of everyone.

When God is on our side, there is no reason or room for fear, whether it be fear of failure, rejection, or abandonment.

Yet Another Fear

Another fear that may be an issue is the fear of men—or, more specifically, people-pleasing. I'd like to believe I don't struggle with this ailment, but the truth is, I do. Most of us do. I have yet to meet someone who says, "I don't care what people think about me," and really means it. Humans are hardwired with a desire to be accepted (i.e., we don't want to be rejected). I feel like this is some of what Moses was dealing with at the moment of His call from God: *"But Moses protested to God, 'Who am I to appear before Pharaoh? Who am I to lead the people of Israel out of Egypt?'"*

In other words, "Why would they listen to me, God? Who am I to appear before these power structures with such a great purpose?"

I have a deep level of understanding of this sentiment. This very thing kept me safely in "my lane" of leading worship for years. Don't get me wrong: I *loved* every bit of my life as a worship leader. My friend Ross King and I would often joke about our dream of becoming "*minor Christian celebrities, almost regionally famous at youth camps with fifteen- to sixteen-year-olds.*"

—

Could it be that the measure of our impact is equivalent to the measure of our obedience?

Before you throw down this book thinking I'm a narcissist, I'm kidding (hence the mocking aspirational title). Seriously, though, when it comes to leading worship, I have loved every minute of it, and I still love to lead when I can, where I can. However, due to my fear of men and my need to please others, I had convinced myself that I lacked the qualifications for a higher level of leadership. I didn't believe I deserved it, nor did I think I would be able to garner the respect of people as their leader, so I stayed away from being a pastor.

The Devil Will Always Try to Derail Your Destiny

God has His desires for our lives, but the devil will always try to derail our destiny! I was convinced I had nothing to offer other than leading people in corporate worship. That's not a secondary calling by any measure, but deep down in my bones, I knew God had more for me to do. In fact, I had known for some time that God wanted more from (and for) me, but who was I willing to truly be obedient to? Could it be that the measure of our impact is equivalent to the measure of our obedience? I knew, in order to truly give God my best yes, it would require:

1. Choosing the path of greater resistance
2. Possibly defying everyone else's opinion of what I was supposed to be doing and who I was supposed to be
3. Willingly embracing, by faith, roles and responsibilities that felt questionable at best (at least to the world around me)

Enter Noah. Enter Abraham. Enter Moses. We see in Exodus 3:13 that Moses may have been struggling with a bit of impostor syndrome.

"What do I tell them, God? What do I tell Pharaoh, God?"

Abraham seemed to struggle with counting the cost as well. Why else would he tell his wife, upon his entering Egypt, to pose as his sister unless he was afraid of what people would say, think, or do? I've said it before, and I'll say it again: If insecurity is the libelous thief of a life of impact, fear is the enemy of faith and fulfillment. It's not that God can't use it—He can use anything—but what are we costing ourselves in time, impact, favor, and obedience when we choose fear over faith?

Another way the enemy tries to derail our destiny is through *comparison.*

Comparison: The Other Killer

Comparison is the thief of vision. Run your race and trust that there is grace for God's pace. Don't waste time looking to the right or to the left. Don't waste time wondering if you are enough, have enough, do enough, etc.

As a friend of mine often says, our God is not a God of "*do better, try harder.*" Our God is the *"It is finished"* kind of God, meaning that He who began the good work in you will be faithful to complete that good work, no matter where your road may lead you, no matter the seasons, storms, twists, and turns. Now, of course, this still requires *your yes*!

—

If insecurity is the libelous thief of a life of impact, fear is the enemy of faith and fulfillment.

When you compare yourself to someone else, you rob God of His creative ability in how He uniquely created you. Not only that, but when you compare yourself to someone else, you call into question God's creativity as it pertains to you as His *Imago Dei*, designed uniquely by Him to become uniquely you!

Through comparison, we potentially abdicate our assignment to the body of Christ as a whole by trying to be someone or something else. God calls us, blesses us with talents and gifts, and "appoints and anoints" us for *our* specific destiny. When it comes to God's plan, path, and purpose for your life, He has made you *more* than enough. Whatever you may feel you lack, God will provide.

—

God has called many people to greatness who didn't feel all that great.

When comparing, we can always find reasons why we don't have enough, or we aren't enough, or someone else is more than enough. But remember, God called *you*. God created *you* for such a time as this. He wants to memorialize His goodness and power through *your* life. It may not be the story Noah, Abraham, Moses, or David lived out, but it's your story, walking obediently with God nonetheless.

At the End of the Day

As we can clearly see through the stories of a faith father (Abraham), a leader (Moses), a king (David), a Samaritan woman, and a eunuch, God has it all under control. It's easy when comparing your life against others to feel like you aren't qualified, are disqualified, or are incapable. It can become second nature to simply assume you have nothing of real substance to offer, so why even consider your potential? I mean, what impact could you have, really?

Be careful not to confuse a low self-image with humility, because that can become a thief of God's vision as well. The root of both is pride. As you contemplate God's call and any step of faith He invites you to take, know that you're in good company.

—

God has uniquely created you to be you.

Along the way, I'll keep reminding you of the company we find ourselves in when following God. God has called many people to greatness who didn't feel all that great. If you find yourself in the comparison game, at least do it like Elisha did. He found a worthy spiritual mentor, Elijah, to follow. I have to believe he was thinking, *God, I do want what Elijah has, and then some. I want a double portion of it, because I want to be my own monument unto Your name!*

Remember, God has uniquely created you to be you. He made you on purpose, for His purpose, and He has something significant that He wants to do in, through, and with your life. The enemy of faith and fulfillment is fear, but the Almighty God is calling us to this monumental life of making an eternal impact!

That counts for everything.

Pray this prayer with me:

Father, would You silence any created voice speaking that I may only hear from the voice of my Creator? Help me believe that You are my validation, the source of my destiny and calling, and that I have nothing to fear in You. In this, also bring Your truth to the giants—the fears of failure, rejection, and abandonment as well as comparison. Once again, meet me in this place, Your holy place, and reveal to me Your passion for my path and Your heart for me.

I pray this in Your mighty Name, Jesus. Amen.

04

ENDURANCE WILL BE ESSENTIAL

Isaiah 30:20–21 (NLT)

Though the Lord gave you adversity for
food and suffering for drink,

He will still be with you to teach you.

You will see your teacher with your own eyes.

Your own ears will hear him. Right
behind you a voice will say,

"This is the way you should go," whether
to the right or to the left.

Storms, Seasons, & Suffering

Before we proceed, it is imperative that I state an undeniable truth: Life in Christ—following Jesus and living as a monument to His goodness—will not be without its wind and waves. Monuments often tell the story of situations where endurance was essential. So will it be on the journey ahead.

Storms will come.

Seasons of wilderness and deserts will come.

Suffering will come. It's not a matter of *if* but *when.*

Moments of grief, trauma, and even tragedy may occur, but that doesn't call into question God's goodness; it only indicts humanity's brokenness. Humanity chose to eat the fruit of the tree of the knowledge of good and evil, and here we find ourselves. Thank God that He chose to make a way through Jesus to redeem the world, and now, it's Jesus who invites us to partner with Him for His redemptive purposes. What a humbling privilege He bestows upon us. The monumental life isn't found in achievement, perfection, or some utopian existence; it's found by walking in obedience to the purposes, plans, and paths that God invites us to, no matter what may come.

I've found that many people want a *platform*, but they don't want the *process.* We want a significant life, but we don't want to struggle for it in any way. However, there is no diamond without pressure, and there is no oil without crushing. When counting the cost of obedience to God's calling, we must know that the story God writes through our lives will involve seasons of suffering.

—

Moments of grief, trauma, and even tragedy may occur, but that doesn't call into question God's goodness; it only indicts humanity's brokenness.

Let me reframe this for us and propose the following: What if suffering's role in our lives is part of our sanctification? What if wilderness moments are part of the way God refines us? What if the dry, desert places are where God faithfully reminds us that He is the source of our living water? What if God uses the storms we face to build our faith and prepare us for His greater purposes? I've learned many times over that because we live in a broken world, suffering is unavoidable—and it can either derail you or define you.

My family has faced some challenges as it pertains to birth stories. My first son, Jadon, cooperated during his grand entrance into the world; it honestly couldn't have gone better. I believe this was the grace of

God for us because the Lord knew my wife and I needed this precedent for what was to come. On the other hand, I began this book by telling you about my third son's more difficult entrance into the world, which was a traumatic journey full of ups and downs, twists and turns. His story changed our lives for the better, for sure, but his first eight years were incredibly difficult. We didn't know what the outcome of his traumatic, premature birth would be. I'm glad to report that today he is a healthy, happy teenager, which is thanks to the supernatural, restorative, and redemptive work of God. The birth story of Jack, my middle son, was also a defining moment for our family.

It was 2005. My wife, Kelly, was twelve weeks pregnant when we arrived on site for an annual summer conference that we lead. That year, our ministry theme was *"All Things New."* Our team had done the exhausting, laborious work of setting up and transforming the campus, and were ready for people to arrive. The stage was set, complete with a thirty-foot-wide, twenty-foot-tall backdrop, bearing a billboard-sized picture of a sonogram and the words "ALL THINGS NEW" plastered across it. That image was the best thing we could think of that conveyed a sense of joy in new life.

The morning the conference was to begin, as we always did, we gathered to pray by name for every person who was registered and on their way. Just as we began to pray, Kelly burst through the back doors of the auditorium, calling my name as she stumbled weakly down the aisle before collapsing. The next few hours would be filled with anxiety and uncertainty, combined with an awakening to spiritual warfare like we had never known.

This particular conference was being hosted on a college campus in a small town in Louisiana, which unfortunately had limited options for medical treatment. After entering the closest hospital we could find and going through a relatively quick triage process to see a doctor, we encountered some unexpected situations. The first thing we noticed after heading back toward an exam room was a literal jail cell in this emergency room, with a sign affixed to its bars instructing visitors to clean up their own refuse. (I'm sorry—what?) For starters, *why* was there a prison cell in this hospital? Where were we? I mean, call me sheltered, but I don't think that's normal, at least not in the types of emergency room settings I had become accustomed to while living in

Houston, which is home to one of the world's premier medical complexes. There we were, hundreds of miles away from home, our conference starting in a few hours, and Kelly was bleeding profusely. There was an obvious issue with our pregnancy, and this was the hospital available to us? En route to the exam room, we crossed paths with a nurse who proudly wore a pentagram necklace, complete with the almost clichéd dark, goth image of black fingernails and lipstick. The staff placed us in a room just past the jail cell to wait for a doctor, gave Kelly a bedpan, and asked us to tell them if we saw something pass other than blood. Please forgive the details, but they are essential to understanding the full scope of the story.

The situation got worse from there.

Upon inspecting the room where they placed us to wait, I saw bloody tools in the sink, presumably left from the prior patient. I almost couldn't process everything I was seeing in real time. I was trying my best to keep my bearings and stay focused on Kelly out of an obvious and grave concern for her and our unborn child; however, I couldn't ignore the sense of darkness all around us in this hospital. At this point in our lives, I don't know what I could have articulated that I fully believed spiritually, but what happened next would fully awaken me to the reality of the demonic attack we found ourselves under. As if on cue, an older woman wheeled by our room in a wheelchair, paused to peer inside, and then pushed our half-closed door open to point at Kelly while saying, "Don't let them wait until you are too old to tell you your body is filled with cancer! I had cervical cancer, and you do too." I immediately moved toward this woman, demanding that she leave our room, and shut the door in her face. I did my best to try to reassure Kelly, despite what had just happened. There was no doubt in my mind that the lady was sent on assignment by the devil to speak a curse over my wife.

For the next few hours, we struggled with the tension between our faith in what God could do and the reports the doctors were giving us. Strangely, amid the chaos and our shock regarding our situation, I felt as though I heard the Lord. However, what I sensed I was hearing seemed almost cruel. To this day, I still can't decide whether I was projecting or prophesying, but what I believed God was bringing to my heart was John 11:4 (NIV), which describes when news had reached

Jesus that Lazarus was gravely ill. Jesus's response? "*This sickness will not end in death. No, it is for God's glory so that God's Son may be glorified through it.*" It felt like a total contradiction to what seemed to be the collision course my wife and I found ourselves on. I struggled with telling Kelly what I felt God was saying for fear of missing something or mishearing the Lord. What if that passage was simply what I *wanted* God to say and do? And, worse—what if He didn't?

What if God uses the storms we face to build our faith and prepare us for His greater purposes?

Most of that day was filled with dismay, grief, despair, desperate prayers for healing, waiting, and a feeling of senseless void. We were in a different state, all set to declare the greatness of God to a conference full of people, but at that moment, nothing felt great. It felt like we were in a bad dream from which we couldn't wake up. What we felt God saying was in *no way* making sense based on what we were seeing.

What our eyes could see was an unimaginable amount of blood coming from a human.

What our ears could hear was the absence of a heartbeat on the fetal monitors during the examinations.

What our eyes could see was a seemingly cruel sonogram picture of our child, whom six doctors declared to be dead that day—a miscarriage.

... But God!

God, being supernatural, isn't limited by our "natural," nor is He limited by any borders or boundaries of our beliefs. He is the all-powerful God who truly can make all things new. This wasn't merely a theme we were to teach transactionally; it was a transformational encounter He wanted us to live out. Even writing this story is picking at some scars and letting some very real, raw emotions resurface. My wife and I had a keen awareness that day that no matter what we saw with our eyes, our reality was a full-fledged, hate-filled demonic attack, to say the least. We can now look back and believe it was God's grace at work. While thoughts like this may feel uncomfortable, I believe God entrusted us with this lesson so that we might deepen our belief in Him and His power, as well as visibly declare that He alone is the God of resurrection, restoration, and redemption.

Late in the afternoon, after strongly suggesting we allow them to perform a D&C, the hospital staff called in a specialist to examine Kelly. They were likely exasperated with me and my adamant stance against their treatment of choice. The specialist, after her initial exam, requested we allow the full battery of usual testing for situations like this, which Kelly had already endured for most of the day. Why not one more time? At this point, there had been a lot of praying and waiting, and the bleeding had subsided. After a blood draw and reading of panels, along with a few minutes of confusion, the specialist requested another sonogram. This is when the miraculous would be made manifest, resulting in a monumental moment neither of us will ever forget. The doctor would have to look at Kelly and apologize in disbelief because, contrary to the lab results recorded earlier in the day that had indicated depleted hormone levels, along with sonograms that did not detect a heartbeat, everything was now different. What had been declared dead earlier in the day was now absolutely alive! What appeared lifeless now revealed a God who was limitless!

—

God, being supernatural, isn't limited by our "natural," nor is He limited by any borders or boundaries of our beliefs.

With everything in me, I believe that day that we did find ourselves in a John 11 (NLT) moment. Just as Jesus declared about Lazarus, "*This will not end in death, but for the glory of God, that the Son of God may be glorified through it,*" I believe He was declaring that promise to us regarding our middle son. I'm happy to report that today, Jack is a thriving nineteen-year-old. He's a stellar, electric-guitar-playing worship leader who has the heart of David. That day, God made *all things new*, as He healed my wife and Jack, bringing him to full-term, while revealing to us His good, mysterious, yet mighty ways.

Make no mistake: This storm, with its wind and waves, shook us to the core. The experience rattled me personally, but it also refined me in ways that would fortify my faith in the God who is, was, and is to come. The God who parted the waters for His people way back in Exodus and at the Jordan was the same God who made a way for my son.

While I know God had a plan in and through it all, I praise God that He only asked us to endure the suffering for that one day. Sure, there were unknowns throughout the rest of Kelly's pregnancy, but that day was one for the record books. I wish I could say I was a pillar of immovable belief at the time, but I wasn't. I did my best to be as strong as humanly possible for my wife, but mentally, I was a mess. It's amazing how God used that moment in our lives, and the lives of many others, to prove He truly does make all things new. I believe my son is a living miracle, a monument to the power and provision of a holy and faithful God. I often think about all God did that day with a deep sense of gratitude and awe, and I can't help but remember it when I look at my son.

I wonder if you can recall a season of suffering you've endured. Surely, the entirety of your life hasn't been one mountaintop experience after another. There have been some valley moments here and there. That's how it goes for all of us, which is why we find a passage like Psalm 23 in the Scriptures (ESV), which says, "Even though I walk through the valley of the shadow of death, I will fear no evil, for You are with me."

You have likely lived long enough to understand the importance of that promise. Like me and many others, I imagine you've faced your own gut-wrenching and heart-pounding situations where circumstances weren't what you would have ordered for yourself. I'm sure there have been days when the pain came in wave after wave and never seemed to relent.

The disciples who walked with Jesus in the flesh were also called to endure hardship, storms, dry seasons, and moments when the anxiety of the assignment may have felt too great for them.

Storms

We see the story of one such storm in Mark 4. It had been a long day of teaching and being surrounded by crowds, and it was getting late, so

Jesus and His gang took off in a boat to cross to the other side of the lake to find reprieve. It wasn't long into their journey before a fierce storm arose.

(Again, don't be surprised that, even when you are walking in total obedience to God's commission on your life, you travel into some storms.)

—

Don't be surprised that, even when you are walking in total obedience to God's commission on your life, you travel into some storms.

The Bible tells us that a fierce storm, complete with strong winds and high waves, caused the boat to begin taking on water. Notice that even with Jesus *on* the boat, the vessel began to take on water. They were being rocked and whipped around, *while Jesus was with them.*

Yes, there will come times in life when the wind whips us and the waves crash against us, and it feels like our boat is taking on water, even though Jesus is right there with us. What has always fascinated me about this story is Jesus's capacity to be sound asleep in the back of the boat, with His head nestled on a cushion, while the disciples are in a full frenzy of fear, freaking out about the wind and the waves.

Some of the disciples finally went to wake Him from His slumber. Here's how it plays out in my imagination:

"Jesus, you gotta wake up!"

"Don't you care we are about to die here, Jesus?"

"Teacher, this ship is about to go down, and all you can do is sleep?"

"Can't you see, or care, that we are all about to drown?"

I can unequivocally, with zero hesitation, tell you that Jesus *does* see, and Jesus *does* care. In fact, He cares *immensely*. I personally know this to be true.

Jesus hadn't called these disciples to such a monumental destiny and led them all that way, just to die there like that. Jesus also didn't come from heaven to earth, abdicating total glory for seeming poverty, to die like that. Yes, He cared, so what did He do? Scripture says that after He woke up, He rebuked the wind and spoke to the waves, demanding them to be silent and still.

When God calls us to live a monumental life, it doesn't mean the absence of suffering or storms, but it does assure us the presence, power, and provision of Jesus.

I'm sure to the astonishment of every disciple on the boat, the wind suddenly ceased, yielding to a great sense of calm. The scene ends with Jesus asking questions as to the reason for their fear, as if to say, "Guys, I'm here. Do you still not believe in me? Do you still not know that I'm with you? Can you not believe I'm able to settle the storm even after you've seen me do even greater things? You have nothing to fear!"

Considering the guy could turn wastewater into fine wine and bend the laws of medical science by healing the way He did—and especially after watching Him deliver someone from demons—surely *that* guy can be trusted. And to think—He was right there in the boat with them!

This truth applies to us as well. When God calls us to live a monumental life, it doesn't mean the absence of suffering or storms, but it does assure us the presence, power, and provision of Jesus. Wind and waves will come. The boat of your life will rock and bend. You'll have moments when it's all too much for you. You'll take on water until it feels like your boat is sinking, but be encouraged: Jesus is on your boat ***with you***.

I posed versions of these questions earlier:

- What if God uses the seasons and storms in our life to sanctify our life?
- What if the journey God calls us to is not as much about a destination or result as it is about a process of refinement?

- What if the process we are called to endure is for a greater purpose?
- What if God leverages those crushing seasons where we face storms, winds, and waves for our preparation?

I believe that with God, nothing is wasted: Neither a season nor a storm. Not the most turbulent of winds or the most treacherous of waves. No mountain and no valley. Nothing. God uses every bit of it: every day, every hour, every moment, every second. There is no storm, season, sifting, or suffering in which God isn't with us and at work.

God's call upon our life will always necessitate His presence.

Remember, God's call upon our life will always necessitate His presence. Accepting God's invitation to the life He has planned for us makes His presence essential! When God calls us, it's for something powerful, impactful, and purposeful that will require the supernatural. What if the storm the disciples encountered that day was nothing more than an exercise? What was there to learn through this storm as they crossed the sea? It seems to me that a true encounter with Jesus is far superior to any encounter you could have with a storm.

What's amazing about the end of the storm story in Mark 4 is that they were terrified and in awe at the power of the weather, but they ended up more reverent and in awe of the power and person of Jesus. Rightly so. We have nothing to fear when Jesus is with us.

Sifting

I've always been fascinated by Peter's story. Here's a young adult, somewhat a misfit, whom Jesus calls to follow Him. He was a fisherman by trade, most likely stepping into the family business. Their first encounter was after Peter had fished all night, desperately needing a large catch so as to pay some debts, and he caught nothing. Jesus instructed him to throw his nets on the other side of the boat. This had to be laughable to Peter, who almost certainly knew what he was doing when it came to fishing. However, as the story goes, the catch was so great that it filled not one but two boats—and began to tear the nets.

Lesson one, Peter: Even when it seems completely hopeless and you feel at your most vulnerable, God's will for your life triumphs over any weakness in your life.

During another moment with Peter, Jesus had led His disciples to a city called Caesarea Philippi. There, Jesus stood between His disciples and many monuments that had been built to honor a myriad of false, pagan gods. Jesus chose this place, called the "gates of hell" by many theologians, to stand in full view of these idols and ask His disciples whom they believed Him to be.

"You are the Messiah, the Son of the living God," Peter responded.

Good answer, Peter. Lesson two: Understanding and declaring Jesus's true identity gives us an understanding of the people Jesus declares *us* to be.

"You are my rock, Peter, and in and through your life I will build my church!"

In that time, builders made structures by stacking stones. Jesus, being a builder Himself, declared Peter to be one of the stones He would use to build His church. In so doing, Jesus shows us that He's not as concerned with the physical monuments built to honor Him as with the spiritual monuments being built to honor Him in and through His people. Jesus had called Peter to follow Him some time before this moment. The path had already seen a few ups and downs and some wind and waves. However, it's here that Jesus revealed the monumental purpose for Peter's life.

Lastly, and most importantly, we read the *#DENIALGATE* story of Peter's life. This fascinating and encouraging account is found in Luke 22 (NLT). Jesus informs Peter, who has been called for an indelible purpose, that Satan had asked to sift him like wheat. Not just Peter would be sifted; Satan had asked Jesus's permission to sift *all* of his disciples like wheat.

As it turns out, to follow Jesus is to potentially endure some sifting seasons, and while this part of the story breaks my brain, it's not the point I want you to see. The real core of this story is what Jesus says next to Peter: *"I have pleaded in prayer for you that your faith should not fail, so when you have repented and turned to me again, strengthen your brothers."*

Wait, *what*? This is one of the most amazing, profound statements Jesus makes to Peter, and it has deeply personal and encouraging ramifications for each and every one of us as we journey toward our monumental calling. We can expect storms, seasons, suffering, and even sifting. With all of that, *please don't miss what Jesus just said!*

Read it again: "I have pleaded in prayer for you that your faith should not fail, so when you have repented and turned to me again, strengthen your brothers." In this, Jesus reveals three important things to Peter:

- I'm with you.
- I'm praying/interceding on your behalf.
- I believe in you.

He's saying, in effect, "In fact, I believe in you so much that when you mess up and miss the mark, I want you to get up, repent, return to me, and get busy again."

Peter misses the point. "Lord, I'll go to prison with you and even die with you, if need be."

Jesus, as lovingly as possible, breaks the news. Peter, before daybreak tomorrow, you will deny me not once, not twice, but three times. You'll act as if you don't even know me. You'll go to great lengths to play the part of something you're not. You'll do things you would never want to do, including cursing at a teenage girl. Sure enough, Jesus was right—He always is. Peter indeed did exactly what Jesus prophesied he'd do, but this still isn't the point I want you to see. The point is this: *We all miss the mark.* We will mess up and succumb to the sting of the sifting at times, but Jesus is always there, praying for us, believing in us, calling us to more and greater things. Jesus is always there, inviting us back—to repent and return, and to get busy again following the call to the monumental life He dreamed for us long before we were even born. I pray that this promise of grace hits you like a ton of bricks right now. Peter was a misfit and a mess, but Jesus saw something monumental in him.

What if Peter had allowed his three-peat denial to define his legacy? What if, in his shame, Peter had run away from Jesus rather than toward Him on the beach that morning, as Jesus was waiting to cook breakfast for him over a charcoal fire? Surely, the smell of that fire would immediately invoke for Peter the memory of the very moments of his denials, since there was also a charcoal fire burning to warm the darkness on the night of denial.

—

There will never be a time when Jesus isn't waiting on the shore of our situation to restore and remind us of the life He created us to live.

As my friend Aubrey Spears once pointed out, "How kind of Jesus, in this intentional moment with Peter, to take him to that very place in his heart and head, so as to forgive and restore each count." Remember what Jesus said to Peter long before? "When you repent and return to me, strengthen your brothers," and here is Jesus, post-resurrection, asking Peter if he loved Him—not once, not twice, but three times. One for each denial. And with each question asked and answered—"Yes Lord, you know I love you"—Jesus lovingly reminds Peter of his created purpose: "Feed my lambs, take care of my sheep, feed my sheep."

We need to allow the mercy of this moment between Peter and Jesus to be applied to our lives as well. Jesus knows what He created us for, and He also knows every challenge we will ever face. Nothing shocks or surprises Him. There will never be a time when Jesus isn't waiting on the shore of our situation to restore and remind us of the life He created us to live.

Peter made mistakes, but still his life would go on to become a memorial to the goodness, grace, and greatness of God. It wouldn't be until Pentecost that Peter would finally and truly understand all that Jesus had called him to. The rest is history, but it greatly impacts our present.

Peter's life, though full of all sorts of seasons, sifting, storms, and suffering, would be leveraged for a glorious legacy—and so can ours.

As I said before, suffering is inevitable, and it can either derail or define us. No matter what storms come and no matter what season or sifting may come, we have the choice to let it shape us or sideline us. Consider the fact that no saint in Scripture ever became instantly effective for God without some measure of pain in their life. As hard as this statement is to accept, I believe one of our faith fathers, A.W. Tozer, was right when he said, "It is doubtful whether God can bless a man greatly until He has hurt him deeply."

—

No matter what storms come and no matter what season or sifting may come, we have the choice to let it shape us or sideline us.

Pastor Ken Werlein, one of my pastors, put it this way: "God forges the character we need for His assignments in the gymnasium of trials." It's not that God delights in inflicting pain upon us; it's that He uses the pain we endure for greater purposes. Suffering, sickness, and sifting can become a school of sorts, preparing us for God's invitations and assignments. We must remember who calls us, who equips and empowers us, who provides for us, and who is with us on our boat as we live our lives with legacy in mind.

We are the monuments Jesus has chosen. It may be that today He is standing between us and the idol monuments of the world, asking us, "Who do you say that I am?" The answer we give does not matter nearly as much as the life we choose to embrace and live, a life of legacy that is a living monument to His Name and glory, regardless of the cost and what may come.

Pray this prayer with me:

Father, would you bring a depth of peace to my soul where there have been storms, sifting, or suffering? Remind me that You are with me on this journey and that the life You have given me and called me to is worth everything that comes with it. Help me believe that You are my peace, protection, and provision. No matter what I may face, reveal Your heart to me, Your heart for me, and draw even nearer, Lord. I need Your presence and power in my life so I can live in Your monumental calling. I pray this in Your mighty name, Jesus. Amen.

05

THE MOTIVATION OF A MONUMENTAL LIFE

Psalm 84:8–10 (NLT)

O LORD God of Heaven's Armies, hear my prayer.

Listen, O God of Jacob. O God, look with
favor upon the king, our shield!

Show favor to the one you have anointed.
A single day in your courts

is better than a thousand anywhere else! I would
rather be a gatekeeper in the house of my God than
live the good life in the homes of the wicked.

The Most Important Question

What comes to your mind first when you hear God's name or the name Jesus? A.W. Tozer once said, "What comes into our minds when we think about God is the most important thing about us." This is a famous and foundational statement. Tozer's point was that how we perceive God—whether we affirm total belief in Him or deny Him—has vast implications regarding who we are as individuals, how we influence others, and the impact we make on this world.

Based upon many situations and experiences I have walked through in ministry, I have embraced the idea that, when standing before the Lord to give account of my life, I would prefer to apologize for making much more of Him than He actually is—rather than have to apologize for teaching or leading anyone into unbelief.

—

What you believe determines how you behave.

Let me give you some context. I believe orthodoxy determines orthopraxy, meaning what you believe determines how you behave. When we believe God to be astoundingly holy and immeasurably good, we can't help but live grateful lives desiring righteousness. In other words, the motivation for living a monumental life is solely and holistically based upon the greatness and fidelity of God, making *Him* the focus of the monument, not ourselves. When we begin to fully appreciate His worthiness, recognizing He is the one who gives us worth, we can't help but surrender to His good plans for our lives. Our challenge today is that our culture has an addiction to offense rather than an appreciation for His grace. In case you haven't noticed, we are not short on opinions and preferences in the American church. Tragically, far too many of us have grown up in, and are gripped by, a pervasive culture of offense, preference, and entitlement. We all too willingly hold on to these things, making us the monument, which should drive us to repent. Yet in the syncretism of this age, we've even chosen to replace repentance with tolerance. This, I believe, has had devastating effects on our theology and has polluted our ability to follow Christ purely and passionately.

Even with the loftiest of intentions, I'm afraid our traditions, thoughts, rules, and rituals have made following Jesus more complicated than it should be. Some people have compromised the majesty of God by diminishing His immeasurable and omnipotent power and ability. There are many religious circles, and certain streams of systematic theology, that have taken an infallible, unchangeable God and ascribed to Him certain limitations and humanistic borders and boundaries. This may be a form of God, but not one worth putting much faith in.

The Bible speaks about this very issue in 2 Timothy 3 (NLT), as Paul warns of a culture of the last days: "They will act religious, but they will reject the power that could make them Godly." Paul actually says to stay away from people that do this.

Some of our theological systems have muddied our doctrine of salvation (soteriology), and certain haughty hermeneutics (interpretations) are causing more and more challenges to a childlike, faith-filled implementation. Make no mistake, I'm in no way suggesting that we should have an immature intellect where faith is concerned. I am saying that more and more, we risk losing intimacy with a holy and powerful God to the idol of theological intellectualism.

God is exceedingly worthy of our most zealous pursuit and study, but simply by the nature of who He is, He will never be fully figured out. With that said, let me unapologetically declare that I could never make enough of God; nor could anyone, for that matter. There is absolutely nothing that God cannot do—He who was, *is*, and forevermore shall be. He stands alone, outside our borders and boundaries, transcendent and limitless in every way.

As Abraham Kuyper once said, "There is not a square inch in the whole domain of our human existence over which Christ, who is sovereign over all, does not cry, 'Mine!'" This includes me and you! Our God is full of might, mystery, and mercy, and this is the God who has an amazing intended purpose for our lives. He invites us into a partnership with Him to accomplish His good plans. He is not only supremely holy but also unfathomably faithful and exceedingly able, worthy of our all. There is no power imaginable that is greater, and this powerful God promises to be our Shepherd and our Source. There is nothing He can't do, and there is no length He hasn't gone for the explicit pursuit of our renewal, restoration, and redemption.

Ephesians 2:10 (NLT) declares that we are His masterpiece, and the reason for Him creating us anew, in and through Christ Jesus, is so we can step into the good things He planned for us long ago. God desires for us to live the abundant life that He dreamed for us!

So what is this monumental life, and why should we feel motivated to give Him our best yes?

A Shift in Thinking

So what do you think about first when you hear the name Jesus? Is there anything God cannot do? What do you believe about God?

Dennis and Patty were pastoring students when they invited me to lead worship for their summer camp, which launched us into a fast friendship. They had the type of passion for Jesus that said "Yes" to Him no matter the ask or cost, and God was working through them and had greatly blessed their obedience.

Those types of people always intrigue me because of the contagious nature of their faith and openhanded availability to God. One day when my wife and I were hanging out with them, Dennis shared a testimony which shook us but inspired us. Dennis described, in great detail, the events that led him to surrender everything to Jesus, and it was nothing short of breathtaking and, honestly, hard to wrap our minds around.

Fair warning: You're about to understand why I asked what you believe about God, and why I explained how I approach my thinking and speaking about God.

Before Dennis met and married Patty, he was driving in his truck with a friend when he came to a curve. A lady in a car was approaching him in his lane, and she overcorrected, which made her lose control of her vehicle and divert toward a ditch. Before Dennis could fully react, her car was propelled out of the ditch and landed sideways in front of him. This caused him to lose control of his truck and sent him flipping end over end, multiple times.

Suddenly, according to Dennis, everything seemed to be happening in slow motion. As his truck was flipping through the air, his friend reached out to him, and he reached for her—only to see her be ejected from his vehicle. Then the truck flipped a few more times, finally coming to stop upside down.

Dennis crawled out, got up, dusted himself off, and began looking around frantically for his friend. He saw her and began to move toward her, but that's when he realized something was off. He became hyperaware of things around him: cars, people, his friend, birds. He seemed compelled to stop and look around, because he realized something wasn't right.

Everything had stopped, as if literally frozen in time. There was an unmistakable eerie stillness and a deafening silence. There were no cars moving or honking—nothing. Birds were literally suspended in midair.

What is happening? Dennis thought. *This can't be possible.*

He moved to check on his friend, and right at that moment, everything started moving again. Horns began honking, car tires were screeching, and the sounds of wreckage ensued. He looked back at the truck he had just crawled out of to see it turn over a few more times, crashing hard. This crushed the cab to a point that no one could have survived.

But Dennis survived, as did his friend.

What. Just. Happened?

This is Dennis's testimony, and he has shared it many times over the years. The details are always the same.

Yes, Dennis looked back at his truck to see it continue rolling, after he had escaped it while it was standing still. *Let that sink in.*

Did the Sun Stand Still?

Was Dennis's experience like in the days of Joshua? In Joshua 10, during a battle against the Amorite kings, Joshua prayed for the sun to stand still so that Israel could finish the fight. God answered, miraculously extending the day until Joshua and his men could defeat all of their enemies. This event, though completely unprecedented, demonstrated God's provision, power, faithfulness, and favor, while affirming Joshua's leadership. And while unimaginable, this act of God's sovereignty, in which the sun stood still, ensured complete victory for Israel.

I know Scripture says that there has never been a day like that one before or since, but how else do you explain something so obviously supernatural? It's as if God pushed the cosmic pause button to create a way for His children in peril at that horrific moment.

It goes without saying that Dennis was in utter shock at the sight of it all. He was completely shaken, yet lucid enough to remember every detail clearly. He walked away from what could only be described as total devastation with only a small mark on his back, and his friend had a small laceration on her leg—that's all.

Clearly, God had specific and significant plans for my friend Dennis. There was an obvious God-created, God-ordained purpose for his life. It's incredible how, in an instant, God can make a way, no matter how supernatural, out of such potential wreckage. How can you explain such an event? It defies comprehension.

Tragically, most people would say such a thing is impossible, or they would explain it as anything but God. Still, there's no real way to describe this story other than to say, "But God!"

—

The abundant life is not a life without adversity, but a life that promises blessing.

Not long after that, Dennis would meet Patty, marry her, and surrender his life to minister to students. Even their call to ministry had a supernatural component. God spoke to Dennis and Patty separately but on the same day, with the same call. Since then, they have known both feast and famine, days of sunshine and rain, and while life hasn't been easy for them, I believe they would testify that it sure hasn't been empty! They have seen God do incredible things, even when they've found themselves in seasons of hardship. God has made a way for them repeatedly where there seemed to be no way.

They have chosen to live a life that is somewhat quiet where crowds are concerned—but loud when honoring the Lord. They've taken slow, methodical, small steps of faith in the same direction daily. That approach can lead you down some rough and rocky roads, but it will always eventually end in a beautiful place.

The abundant life is not a life without adversity, but a life that promises blessing. With all that said, the monumental life is a long journey, taking the daily steps in the same faithful and faith-filled direction, planting seeds with each step, and living with legacy in mind. This journey is well worth any seasons of wilderness we may walk through, and simply by virtue of who God is, it is a life definitively worthy of the One who is with us and for us every step of the way.

How Did We Get Here?

Hearing extraordinary stories like Dennis and Patty's is always encouraging if your heart can allow your head to believe that God is sometimes undefinable in His supernatural and transcendent existence. He can and does work in supernatural ways for significant reasons. Kelly and I came away from Dennis's story wide-eyed, feeling inspired and full of faith and hope. We adopted a unified desire to make ourselves completely available to God, and we committed to the kind of faith that says yes, no matter what God asks.

Our deepest hope is that one day, after a long journey of walking step by step in the same radical, faith-filled direction toward God's desires, we will look up and not fully understand how we arrived at our destination—but be grateful. It's not that we're against strategic planning, not at all. It's just that we are joyfully aware that our best plans can never compete or compare with what God has designed for us.

Our deepest desire is that our story will be part of a greater script, one that can only be scribed by a supernatural and sovereign God. We want to live that Abraham kind of faith (with one caveat: We'd rather not have children at the spry age of one hundred! Praise Jesus He didn't wait that long to bless us with kids!). When all is said and done, our heart is that of Ephesians 3:20 (NLT), which says, "Now all glory to God, who is able, through his mighty power at work within us, to accomplish infinitely more than we might ask or think."

What about you? What do you desire for your life? Is anything stopping you from giving God your best yes to the significant life He desires and has planned for you?

The Monumental Life Defined

What is this monumental life I speak of? At the risk of sounding contrarian, let me begin by establishing what it is not. The monumental life isn't necessarily found in accomplishment, accolades, or affluence. It's not about how much money you can acquire, how many followers you can amass, or how much professional influence you can achieve. I used to believe that to live a significant, purpose-filled life, I would have to ascend onto bigger platforms and sell more music (when I was a worship leader). Oh, yes, and I believe I mentioned that I once dreamed of being a minor Christian celebrity, almost regionally famous with fifteen-year-old students at youth camps. I'm only sort of kidding about that.

I had *big dreams* that involved a busy schedule, broad influence, and a big bank account. While those dreams aren't necessarily bad things, they make for bad gods—consider any celebrity you see on TMZ.

The truth is, the monumental life is significant not because of anything you can do or become; the monumental life is significant because of the engagement of God's upside-down Kingdom. That's the place that declares things like "The last shall be first," "To find life you must lose it," and "No one can serve two masters." Upon tasting God's goodness, giving Him our yes, and embracing His will and ways, we begin to awaken to the abundance of His greatness. I submit to you that the monumental life is found not in our *doing*, or our *becoming*, but simply in our *being*. It's the sacrificial life we willingly live, walking with Jesus, faithfully living our lives as a reflection of His goodness and grace, while choosing to be obedient to His invitations and assignments.

The monumental life begins by giving God our fervent and faith-filled yes, no matter what He may ask of us. After all, there is nothing more motivating than His manifest presence and power working in and through our lives. When we embrace life in Christ and realize our identity in Him, everything changes in the best way possible. It's in the dying of self that we begin to find true life. It's not about living a good life for the attention, applause, or recognition of people, but rather as a memorial of remembrance to the goodness of God. Remember, our lives are a significant part of a greater story God is telling the world, which is ultimately *His* story! Personally, I don't want the culmination of my life to only represent some reputation I build for myself; I want God to use my life to bring revival to the world!

We must be careful not to build monuments to ourselves. We see this happen in the Bible a few times. King Saul, in 1 Samuel 15, had led Israel to attack the Amalekites, as God instructed. However, due to delayed obedience (or partial obedience, which is still disobedience), Saul failed to honor what God explicitly told him to do. He allowed the Amalekite king to survive, and he kept the spoils of the Amalekites' best resources and animals, though God had specifically instructed him to destroy it all. Following his victory, Saul erected a monument, not dedicated to God for His protection or provision but in recognition of himself.

—

The monumental life is significant not because of anything you can do or become; the monumental life is significant because of the engagement of God's upside-down Kingdom.

Absolom did the same in 2 Samuel 18:18. With no heir, he built a monument to himself to ensure the remembrance of his name. At the beginning of Genesis 11, we see God's people do the same. Verse 4 (in the NIV) reveals that they, in their pride, said to each other, "Come, let us build ourselves a city with a tower that reaches to the heavens so that we make a name for ourselves; otherwise, we will be scattered over the face of the whole earth." Tragically, by building this monumental tower to themselves, the very thing they had hoped to avoid in the scattering is the very thing they invited upon themselves.

Because of this, we should ask ourselves some questions daily, especially in light of what Jesus said in Luke 9:23 (NLT): "If any of you wants to be my follower, you must give up your own way, take up your cross daily, and follow me." Questions like these:

- Who am I living to please—God or man?
- Am I living with the end in mind, meaning if I died soon, what legacy would my life leave behind?

- What am I building my life for?

The Tension Of It

We live in this tension. We can all too easily find ourselves proverbially leaning our ladder against the wrong walls and erecting monuments to ourselves, rather than to God. In that scenario, we focus on building our reputation, our brand, and a secular kingdom instead of representing and reflecting God and building His Kingdom.

—

When we embrace life in Christ and realize our identity in Him, everything changes in the best way possible.

Think about the strange world we live in, dominated by duck-faced selfies and social media influencers who promote a specific hyper-filtered version of themselves, selling a lifestyle of fulfillment that is, in actuality, nothing more than a facade. Don't you want to be a part of a monumental move of God, ushering in a great revival for His glory and for the good of the world? When all is said and done, do you want to be remembered for something you've attained or accomplished, or do you want your life to be remembered as a faithful reflection of the love, goodness, and power of God?

I'll never forget the first time I saw global media coverage of people who had lived under the weight of tyranny, now exuberantly declaring victory and freedom. It was April 2003, nearly a year to the day that Saddam Hussein had erected a thirty-nine-foot statue of himself in the center of Firdos Square in the heart of Baghdad as a monument to his own greatness. An Iraqi insurgency combined with American forces brought an end to Saddam's rule in Iraq, an event that people celebrated in jubilant style with songs, dancing, and the destruction of the idol built in honor of the now fallen leader.

After the statue was toppled, it was decapitated, and the freed people dragged the head through the streets so that everyone could see and celebrate their liberation. The reign of the despotic tyrant was finally over, and the Iraqi people began to taste freedom.

Idols and monuments built to anything or anyone other than God brazenly celebrate the pride of man outwardly, while inwardly memorializing a lack of true freedom. The Apostle Paul once lived a life of influence, recognition, and affluence, but later, he would boldly declare "to live is Christ, and to die is gain" (Philippians 1:21 NIV). After his encounter with the glory of God on the road to Damascus, Paul would have violently pulled down any monument he may have previously wanted to build for himself, so as to embrace the truth of Jesus. As we read in Matthew 10:39 (NLT), "If you cling to your life, you will lose it; but if you give up your life for me, you will find it."

This verse illustrates the upside-down nature of the Kingdom of God. Choosing to focus on things like worldly ambitions or personal gain will lead to a loss of true, abundant life. On the other hand, a life dedicated to the glory of God—sacrificing yourself for faith and following Jesus—will lead to a monumental life like no other.

Libertas

This concept is a challenge for us, especially us Americans. We applauded that moment when Saddam's statue was toppled, but we Americans have our own statues and monuments. Many, on the surface, appear righteous. Consider our most famous monument, the Statue of Liberty. One could make a case that this important monument is a symbol that declares a virtuous ethos attached to a Godly value, epitomizing a country birthed with Godly intentions. Lady Liberty proudly welcomes people from around the world into New York's harbor.

—

Idols and monuments built to anything or anyone other than God brazenly celebrate the pride of man outwardly, while inwardly memorializing a lack of true freedom.

However, a deeper dive reveals something which should give us pause, as author Jason Hood so eloquently warned in his book *Imitating God in Christ*:

"Many Americans are unaware that the image atop the base is a Roman goddess named Libertas. We may not worship this image in a traditional religious sense, but it is not too much to say that American allegiance to self, freedom, and independence often becomes a sort of worship. And if we worship these ideals, we become increasingly enslaved to them and unable to serve a God who calls us to discipline, community, and dependence on him. We become undependable, unreliable, radically disconnected and unable to depend on others, just as others cannot depend on us. The same independence that can be a source of blessing can become a god whose worship has horrific effects on the fabric of family, vocation, and culture. Libertas offers self-indulgence and freedom, but she is a cruel mistress, providing only isolation, loneliness, and self-absorption for the individual who clings to independence and rejects the service of God, the constraints of Christian community, or the intimate ties of Christian friendship."[1]

Kelly and I have spent some time in New York, and we've seen this statue in person. Without knowing what the statue truly represents, it's easy to get swept up in awe and emotion, feeling a love and gratitude for the country God has given to us, which is so welcoming to those in pursuit of freedom and a better life. Flawed as she is, the United States of America is still an alluring beacon of hope to a world desiring true liberty. However, while Lady Liberty symbolizes a *version* of freedom, it still in no way memorializes the kind of freedom the soul was created for and craves.

The only monument that can express that holistic type of freedom is the living monument Paul speaks of in Ephesians 2, when he talks of those who have been raised from death to life along with Christ and seated with Him in the heavenly realms through our unity with Him. Paul describes those who have had a "But God" encounter that has changed everything for them. He then goes on to say in verse 7 (NLT) that, "God will point to us in all future ages as examples of the incredible wealth of His grace and kindness toward us, as shown in all He has done for us who are united with Christ Jesus."

[1] Jason B. Hood, *Imitating God in Christ: Recapturing a Biblical Pattern* (Downers Grove, IL: IVP Academic, 2013), 19.

I hope your heart is beating fast at the thought that God desires to point to your life, devoted to Him, as a living monument of His goodness and glory. This isn't because of certain behaviors. It's about specific belonging. Those who truly love and follow Jesus reflect the truth of the love and greatness of Jesus. God, pointing to us, is a proud Father who points at His child, not because of what His child can do, but simply because that child belongs to Him!

The fact that God wants us as His living monuments speaks of a significant life, full of purpose and meaning, that memorializes the miracle of resurrection and redemption, which are only found in and through Jesus.

What an incredible God.

What a mind-blowing invitation He offers us.

When we consider the ramifications of the gospel, the Kingdom of God, and the kindness and goodness of Christ, what more could motivate us and what more could we desire but to live as a monument to the greatness of His Name?

Pray this prayer with me:

Father, my soul's sole desire is that I may live as a pleasing, living sacrifice, devoted to the greatness of Your Name. Lord God, there is truly none like You, for You alone are worthy of the sum of creation's praise and worship. As the Psalm declares, so does my heart: Truly, better is one day in Your courts, one day in Your house, one day in Your presence compared to thousands elsewhere. What a privilege to be Yours, and to live as a living testimony of Your goodness. May my life declare You to be faithful and worthy in every way. Thank You for giving me a place of belonging, meaning, and purpose. As I live to imitate You, may my life honor and memorialize Your great Name in every way.

I pray this in Your mighty Name, Jesus. Amen.

06

MONUMENTS THAT HAVE MATTERED

Psalm 77:11–12 (NLT)
But then I recall all you have done, O Lord;
I remember your wonderful deeds of long ago.
They are constantly in my thoughts.
I cannot stop thinking about your mighty works.

Concrete

I remember the day well. Blue skies, mild breeze—it was in the small gap between a Texas spring and summer when my dad passed away. Upon the arrival of his tombstone, I'll never forget standing there, staring at it.

Kenneth M. Sherrill
March 5, 1941–May 5, 1998

I couldn't seem to look away from that cold concrete block that was putting a declarative exclamation point to an ending. How does something so valuable, something so meaning-filled, so significant just...stop? The concrete block at the head of his resting place, now bearing his name, could never capture or commemorate who this man was, especially to me.

At the risk of sounding like a cliché, I was fixated on the dash between the dates. Now, I'm sure you've heard messages from pastors talking about "the dash," so I won't insult your intelligence. However, *that* dash on *that* memorial stone represented the immeasurable meaning of nearly twenty-four years of my life, and I could not escape the sight of it.

I had lost family members before. I had done the funerals, sung the songs, read the Scriptures, and grieved, but this was different. This one required me to dig deep into the reservoirs of whatever faith I could find inside and hang on for dear life. I was already traveling and ministering when my dad passed away, and I was about to have to leave for a full summer of ministry, while processing his loss in real time.

God met me in those days with such comfort and grace, with a level of kindness I'm not sure I had ever experienced up to that point. I knew the headstone that stood at the place where my dad was buried would soon be lost in a sea of similar headstones, rendered coldly impersonal and easily forgotten in a few generations, but God began to speak to me in a profound way through my grieving process. And what He said so clearly was this: "It's not about the monument built to or for the man; it's about the man the monument is built for."

Let me say that again.

It's not about the monument built to the man; it's about the life of the man the monument is built for.

My earthly father, while not perfect, loved God, worshipped Jesus, loved the church, adored my mom, and was faithful, determined, hardworking, and worthy of the words "well done," in every way. I don't say these things with some romanticized, reimagined version of him in my head. That is who my dad authentically was. He was a great father, husband, friend, brother, and son. Although he experienced sickness and suffering for most of his adult life, he lived a life well worth adoration and emulation. My mom, who is a Godly monument and incredible example in her own right, would attest to this. My sister and I had a great earthly father who did the best he could to represent to us an even greater heavenly Father.

I hope that my "dash" one day, scribed on the concrete of my headstone, can even come close to the dash on his.

Monuments are, by design, to be looked upon for the purpose of remembrance, encouragement, and education.

It has been a long time since my dad went to rest with Jesus. Twenty-seven years now at the time of this writing. I've now lived longer without his presence in my life than I got to live with him, but he made an indelible mark on me, and that impact lives on—in and through my life. While I would never say I've arrived by any measure, there's so much about who I am today that comes from him and the kind of person he taught me to be. I hope anyone who knew my dad could not only say that I look a bit like him but also that my life reflects who he was.

His life mattered to many, especially to my family and me. If there are any steps I take that lead to making an impact on this world, or if there is any good I may do in this life, it can be traced back to the way my parents' faith impacted me. This is why that dash on Dad's headstone gripped me. The monument that stands in the place where my dad was laid to rest matters deeply because of the life it represents. The actual monument is not the concrete slab bearing his name; the true monument was, and always will be, the living memorial to the greatness of God, fully displayed in and through my dad's life and death.

Monuments are, by design, to be looked upon for the purpose of remembrance, encouragement, and education. Unlike anything else in all creation, God made it so our lives can become monuments that others look upon for all those purposes—but even more so, to see His glory. As we've already discussed, in Ephesians 2, God points to His living monuments in future ages that people can look upon, to learn more about who He is and how to rightly follow Him. Paul understood this well. In his newfound identity, purpose, and calling, though he had abdicated the world's version of leadership, he makes a bold declaration in 1 Corinthians 11:1, saying, "Do as I do, for I am doing as Christ did" (paraphrased).

—

God's invitation is to mold our lives into a meaningful, living monument, devoted to the remembrance of who He is.

In fact, he said this multiple times, in different situations, to many people. Paul had counted the cost and willingly chose to embrace the cross in such a way that he would live his life worthy of his calling and of emulation. He also called everyone under his pastoral care to the same pursuit.

We see this in 2 Corinthians 1:1–3. After testifying about how God was using him and his co-laborers to open doors wide for the gospel, he then, with sober humility, talks about the terrific responsibility of carrying a message with such life-altering gravity. Afterward, he encourages the church in Corinth to continue living their lives in humility and holiness, as Godly examples:

> Does it sound like we're patting ourselves on the back, insisting on our credentials, asserting our authority? Well, we're not. Neither do we need letters of endorsement, either to you or from you. You yourselves are all the endorsement we need. Your very lives are a letter that anyone can read by just looking at you. Christ himself wrote it—not with ink, but with God's living Spirit; not chiseled into stone, but carved into human lives—and we publish it. (MSG)

Did you catch what Paul just put down? Our lives are a letter that can be read simply by observing us. God is scripting our story, through His Holy Spirit, faithfully and miraculously marking our lives in a tangible and visible way with His glory, for others to see. Shout it from the rooftops: Our lives, and how we live unto the Lord, greatly matters! Who we are informs the world around us of who God is. This can have both positive and negative implications, depending on how we represent God.

Oh, that we would represent Him so incredibly well! Oh, that we would gratefully reflect His greatness, because of how much it matters. God's invitation is to mold our lives into a meaningful, living monument, devoted to the remembrance of who He is, which others will look upon for encouragement and education.

Remembrance

Memories are a powerful thing. God has uniquely created us with senses that not only help inform us about the world but also can trigger memories like nothing else. Think about it. How often do certain sights, songs, or smells instantly recall a memory, transporting you back to a specific moment? I can't hear REO Speedwagon trying to "*fight that feeling any longer*" without immediately being thrust back in sixth grade, working out my adolescent but paramount relationship issues. Yes, I know it was sixth grade and all, but listen, our middle school love woes were difficult and demanding. That was back when we called dating "going with" people. My dad would always ask, "Where are y'all going?"

All joking aside, remembrance is a gift and tool God has given us. *Zakhar* is a Hebrew word that means "to remember." In her book and Bible study *Jesus and Women*, author Kristi McLelland offers an interesting perspective on Hebrew culture. She states, and I paraphrase, that unlike our culture in which remembrance involves looking back, to the Hebrews, remembrance was considered a "forward-moving practice." That's what monuments do: They call and convict us to remember. Not only do they memorialize a moment in the past, they also truly encourage and educate us in a way that helps us make decisions in the here and now. Monuments matter because the story they tell shapes the way we think, live, and believe.

Monuments matter because the story they tell shapes the way we think, live, and believe.

From the beginning, God's people built monuments for the purposes of worship, remembrance, information, and instruction. Noah established this practice, but to this day, humanity continues to build monuments for many of the same reasons. Monuments speak to the generations that follow about something significant, whether good or bad. Take the 9/11 museum, for example. My wife and I, on our last visit to New York, visited that museum for the first time. I walked the somber halls, evaluating the exhibits, absorbing as much as I could emotionally handle. I found myself immediately taken back to the horror of that morning.

On September 11, 2001, I was awakened by my sister calling in full panic, asking me what was happening. I recall turning on the television and sitting for hours, glued to the news as it unfolded. The sights and sounds, replayed countless times, were seared into my consciousness. Even after twenty-four years, standing in that place was overwhelmingly poignant, as I was hearing and seeing it all on repeat, which forced me to feel the weight of the tragedy all over again.

This monument, spanning many acres, raises paradoxical thoughts and emotions. Though I understand why it was necessary, I struggled with how much of the memorial highlighted those who had committed such horrendous acts. These people were the reason for such tragedy, so they had to be part of telling the story. However, the monument stands not for the radicalized criminals, but in remembrance of the innocent thousands who lost their lives that day. While each lost person's story is told, the collective stories combined convey a much larger narrative with a singular sense of purpose, greater than any individual.

The 9/11 memorial matters because it will speak to future generations of a resolve, a hope, and a power in a unified people who resolved together to overcome the worst of atrocities. It implores viewers not to lose heart but to continue to have faith in any sense of good that can be found in humanity. While the memorial is not necessarily devoted to anything spiritual, there was certainly a spiritual and sacred element to many testimonies of those lost that day. I left that solemn place mourning it all again, yet also strangely inspired with a renewed sense of love and loyalty for our country, as well as a renewed sense of genuine care for humanity. It's impossible to stand at those fountains of remembrance, seeing the names of each person lost, and not hurt deeply for the countless families affected.

I believe this is why the Israelites had such appreciation for *zakhar.* Not only did monuments matter to them for joyful or somber remembrance, they also encouraged people to continue moving forward, informed and inspired. There's another Hebrew word to consider, which we see at least twenty-four times peppered throughout the Old Testament. The word is *zikrown*, which means a memorial, a record (a memorable thing, day, or writing), or a memento. In Scripture, we often see the Israelites use stones as their mementos. To God's people, the stones told stories passed down from generation to generation as a means of both instruction and encouragement.

Claude Mariottini elaborates:

> The people of ancient Israel set up standing stones ("massebah," *Hebrew*) as memorials and witnesses of God's work in the life of the nation, and in the life of individuals. These monuments are associated with historical events such as deliverance in times of war, divine manifestation to individuals, and significant religious occasions.[2]

An example of this would be what are known as Gezer's standing stones, which have stood for three thousand years at the site of what was one of the largest Canaanite temples in Israel. Many Biblical fathers of faith used stones for the purpose of *zikrown*, including Jacob, Moses, Joshua, and Samuel, to name a few. In 1 Samuel 7:12 (NLT), Samuel set up a memorial stone to commemorate God's faithfulness and intervention. The text says, "Samuel took a large stone and placed it between the towns of Mizpah and Jeshanah. He named it Ebenezer (which means 'the stone of help'), for he said, 'Up to this point the LORD has helped us!'" Samuel's desire was for God's people to, personally and corporately, never forget to praise God for the blessing of His provision, while keeping the remembrance of that blessing in mind for potential future hardships.

[2] Claude Mariottini, "Standing Stones in the Old Testament," *Claude Mariottini – Professor of Old Testament* (blog), September 20, 2021. https://claudemariottini.com/2021/09/20/standing-stones-in-the-old-testament/.

Stories in the Stones

After sensing God's challenge when visiting the Haystack monument, I became fixated on the story of Joshua leading God's people into the Promised Land. That story greatly inspired the messaging of this book. The land promised long ago to Abraham for God's people was now imminent, but the Israelites had one last major faith-requiring hurdle: getting across the Jordan River. Isn't it just like God to invite us into plans and purposes and then require His supernatural intervention?

—

Isn't it just like God to invite us into plans and purposes and then require His supernatural intervention?

Crossing the Jordan to take possession of the promise would be no easy feat; the Jordan had reached flood status and was overflowing its banks at the time. Imagine being a part of that moment. Four hundred and thirty years have passed since God's promise to Abraham, and there has been much hardship and testing, including a difficult season of slavery, scarcity of resources, surrounding opposition, and even years of wandering around lost in the wasteland. Finally, here you are, at the precipice of taking possession of this generational and covenantal promise, and *now this?* Would you believe, after all the challenges you've come through, you now have to deal with a twenty-mile-long, two-mile-wide, 120-foot-deep watery barricade?

After cleansing themselves and carrying out specific instructions involving the Ark of the Covenant, the Israelites once again experienced a miraculous and supernatural intervention from God, as He parted the waters much like He did during the Exodus, allowing His people safe passage across a dry riverbed into the Promised Land. A few notable things took place during this momentous moment. First, it wasn't until the feet of the priests carrying the Ark touched the waters that those waters began to part. Much like Abraham's journey, I believe God initiates but invites us to take the step of faith prior to revealing His plan and provision.

Secondly, the priests were carrying the Ark of the Covenant, which represented the presence of the God of all creation in their midst.

God had been with His people the whole time, and now He revealed to them in dramatic fashion that He was once again with them, going before them, and making a way for them where there seemed to be no way.

In Joshua 4 (NLT), the scene opens after all of God's people have safely crossed over. God instructs Joshua in that moment to choose twelve men, one representing each of the tribes of Israel. In verse 3, God instructs Joshua, "Tell them, 'Take twelve stones from the very place where the priests are standing in the middle of the Jordan. Carry them out and pile them up at the place where you will camp tonight.'"

Joshua did as he was told, and each of the men went into the middle of the river, in front of the Ark of the Lord, picked up their stone, and carried it on their shoulder to build a memorial. In verses 6 and 7, Joshua tells these leaders, "We will use these stones to build a memorial. In the future your children will ask you, 'What do these stones mean?' Then you can tell them, 'They remind us that the Jordan River stopped flowing when the Ark of the Lord's Covenant went across.' These stones will stand as a memorial among the people of Israel forever."

There was a story in the stones worthy of remembrance. It was God who not only enabled their deliverance but also delivered on His promise. It was God who provided in the wilderness, while also providing in the war. Joshua knew the significance of the moment and demanded that they memorialize those miraculous moments so generation after generation could look upon that monument and remember. The stories in the stones testify to a good God, who always makes good on His promises and always provides for His plans and purposes.

We can glean some great truth from the stories in those stones as well. To paraphrase author Kristi McLelland, when we come to a place or a time when we aren't sure where to go or what to do next, pause and look back. Remember how the Lord met us, directed us, and provided for us in those past times.[3]

[3] Kristi McLelland, *Jesus and Women* (Lifeway Church Resources, 2020).

The Israelites had it right with their concepts of *zakhar* and *zikrown*. Much as they remembered God's faithful record in their lives, which encouraged them to keep going, when we remember God's faithful provision in our lives, it gives us courage to trust Him in the unknown and live forward.

Monuments of Meaning

It's almost as if a monument is an echo of God's voice, an instant replay of God's movement, which can edify us and compel us to continue forward in faith, step by step.

Each faith step we take is mission-critical for the assignments God calls us to. The imperfect yet faithful journeys of Noah, Abraham, Isaac, Jacob, Moses, and Joshua serve as powerful examples. They, as Eugene Peterson once said, embarked on "the long, slow faithful journey in the same direction."

My dad did this, and I am committed to doing the same.

It was almost immediately after the loss of my dad that God, in His faithfulness and care for me, sent a Godly man as a mentor into my life at just the right moment. Thanks to an additional invitation amid an already crowded calendar of ministry events, I met Greg and Sherry Webster. My faith was shaken in the immediate aftermath of my dad's passing, and my emotional state was probably not in the best place to continue traveling and ministering as heavily as I was in those days. Still, this invite was more providential than anything. God knew exactly what He was doing in connecting me to Greg at that time.

Each faith step we take is mission-critical for the assignments God calls us to.

While he was not my biological father, Greg stepped into my world and quickly chose to embrace me and love me as if I were his son. He has always had a Spirit-led discernment for people in pain—and a heart like Jesus to minister to their needs. His care in my life picked up where my dad left off, offering me fatherly support, guidance, encouragement, sometimes correction, and wisdom. It was the kindness of God amid my grief that gave me yet another example of authentic faith in action. Greg, like my dad, quickly became a pillar in my life. In no way would he ever allow me to coast or compromise; to this day, he is always ready to encourage or challenge me. I can often hear his voice in my mind, quoting biblical axioms to me: "John, to him whom much is given, much is required. Never forget."

Much like my dad, Greg has been a monument in my life that deeply matters and an incredible example of what it looks like to live a faith-filled life, a memorial to the greatness of God. It's not that Greg's life has been perfect and pain-free, but he has proven himself faithful time and again by living an example worthy of emulation. He committed himself long ago to the slow, faithful journey, taking steps of faith-filled obedience to God in the same direction, always planting seeds, and he has become a faith hero to me. Much like the biblical characters mentioned above and much like my dad, Greg stands as a monument in the hall of faith I look to for encouragement.

True significance begins in the "seeds and steps."

More than stones to tell their stories, it was the lives of these faith heroes that became monuments to the goodness and glory of God, telling a greater story about Him.

Remember, true significance begins in the "seeds and steps."

Seeds and Steps

There's an old aphorism that says, "You can count the apples on the tree, but who can count the apples in a seed?" As Pastor Travis Agnew once said, "So it is with the influence of a single person." We can never underestimate the small, daily steps we take in faith and obedience, and likewise, we can never underestimate the power of each step taken when seen as a seed. Consider the sequoia seed, typically the size of a flake of oatmeal. Who could imagine such a small seed, over time, growing into a tree three hundred feet tall?

Or consider the dramatic changes caused by movement in the tectonic plates located in the earth's lithosphere. The earth has a thin, solid outer shell divided into large plates that fit together like puzzle pieces. These plates float slowly due to convection currents on the earth's foundational mantle, a thick layer of hot, flowing rock. When the plates diverge, converge, or slide past one another, amazing things happen: earthquakes, tsunamis, volcanic eruptions, and even the formation of mountain ranges.

As you faithfully embrace and engage God's plan, your life is being formed into a mountain and a monument to His Name.

Spiritually, this is exactly what I pray to happen in and through your life. As you faithfully give God your daily yes, the seeds and steps of faith over a long time in the same direction will eventually shift the spiritual plates under the surface, which could cause a tsunami of God's glory to hit the shores of everything and everyone around you. Not only that, but as you faithfully embrace and engage God's plan, your life is being formed into a mountain and a monument to His Name. May the result of your faithful obedience to God cause tidal waves of His love and power to continue, wave after wave, leaving an aftermath of legacy for generations to come!

Passion, Purpose, & God's Powerful Plans

Edward Kimball wasn't a celebrity. Honestly, we don't know very much about him. He was most likely a typical, average, everyday guy, but he was also a man with a passion for God and the gospel. His story is quite honestly one to be revered.

It was 1855 in Boston. Kimball was a young Sunday school teacher who was deeply passionate about seeing every one of his students come to the saving knowledge of Jesus. One particular young man in his church class, who worked at the local shoe store, became his mission. Kimball would seek him out at the store, meeting him as he stocked shelves, so they could have important, life-altering, and world-changing conversations.

In this way, Kimball was faithfully and diligently taking steps of faith to "plant the seed." Out of reverence for Jesus and a love for his students, he would introduce this shoe clerk to the Lord. The young man's name was Dwight Lyman Moody.

You may recognize that name, even if you aren't super familiar with his story. D.L. Moody grew into a prolific and prominent evangelist and created several Christian institutions for training. Moody's ministry led to revolutionizing the ministry of a man named Frederic Meyer, which in turn led J. Wilbur Chapman to respond to God's call upon his life. J. Wilbur Chapman grew into an effective evangelist who ended up discipling a man named Billy Sunday. Sunday went on to become a profound evangelist who eventually led thousands of people to Jesus.

And thanks to the inspiration of Billy Sunday, preaching at a crusade in Charlotte, North Carolina, a group of guys dedicated their lives to reaching their city for Christ. Their devotion inspired them to invite an evangelist named Mordecai Ham to come and hold services. The year was 1932, and a young, sixteen-year-old Billy Graham would find his way into the services, sitting mesmerized by what he was hearing.

Eventually, Graham would surrender his life to the calling of the Lord, and the rest is history. Billy Graham went on to become the most influential Christian leader of the twentieth century, preaching to over 215 million people who attended at least one of his four-hundred-plus crusades, where more than 2.2 *million* people responded to the saving knowledge of Jesus Christ.

While most people would focus on Billy Graham in this story, can I submit to you that we would not have Billy Graham's ministry without Edward Kimball's obedience and faith? It was the seeds planted, the steps of faith taken, and the long journey in the same direction by a man who never knew celebrity that led to the most powerful ministry of the twentieth century, which would usher in a revival in a way the world had never seen (and hasn't seen since).

Traps vs. Truth

This is why it's so important not to lose focus on the true definition of a monumental life. It's easy to fall into the temptation or trap of performance, embracing a "do better, try harder," achievement-driven mindset. As I stated in the last chapter, the monumental life isn't necessarily found in accomplishment, accolades, or affluence. It's not about how much money you can acquire, how many followers you can amass, or how much professional influence you can achieve. The monumental life is found in the seeds planted and the steps of faith taken. It's the long, slow journey, step by step, in the same direction, obedient to God's desires, invitations, and assignments.

—

The monumental life is found in the seeds planted and the steps of faith taken. It's the long, slow journey, step by step, in the same direction.

If we want our life to truly count, if we want to make a deep and indelible impact and leave a legacy, it won't be because of any power we may have, platform we may stand on, or promotion we may achieve. It will be because we've chosen, like Paul, to take that lesser traveled, narrow road of humility—dying to self and carrying our cross, so as to follow Jesus daily in whatever it is He asks of us. The seeds we plant and the steps of faith we take in obedience lead to a significant, monumental life that matters.

What a privilege it is, what an honor, that God invites us to live as a memorial to His goodness and greatness! And who knows? God may use us like He used Kimball. What an amazing thought that one day, in the new Jerusalem, He may share with us how each faith step we took, and each seed we planted, made a significant impact in the lives of millions—or in the life of just one. Either way, whatever impact we make will continue to have ripple effects for generations to come! Thanks, and praise be to God!

Pray this prayer with me:

Father, I pray for the faith and obedience to focus on the seed and the steps. Take my life and do with it as You please. Make me into a monumental, meaningful memorial of remembrance, unto Your Name alone! May the stones I stack be the steps of faith and obedience I take, so they speak loudly to future generations of Your goodness, Your faithfulness, and Your power and provision. I know that when I am living rightly in Your invitations and assignments, You can do abundantly more than I can ask, think, dream, or imagine! Have Your way, Lord! Amen.

07

OPPORTUNITIES TO BE AN OFFERING

> 1 TIMOTHY 6:12 (MSG)
>
> Run hard and fast in the faith. Seize the eternal life, the life you were called to, the life you so fervently embraced in the presence of so many witnesses.

Life...from Death?

Though nearly twenty-eight years ago now, it wasn't long before my dad passed that God brought my attention to that verse I spoke of earlier, Galatians 2:20. I'm sure I had read it before and probably heard some sermons about it at some point. However, this time it felt like this verse seized me for the first time and spiritually punched me square between the eyes.

What was so profoundly gripping about reading Paul's words—"I've been crucified with Christ, and it is no longer I who live"—was that I knew that through them, God was speaking directly to me, and that this passage would likely determine the rest of my life, if I embraced the call. I also knew there was no other option but to accept the dying of "self" and the crucifixion of my ideals, dreams, control, entitlement, and agenda, because that is what Jesus prescribed for everyone who would truly follow Him.

—

It's in the dying of self that embracing God's design and desires for our life begins.

Here's the kicker: I didn't even have verses like Ephesians 3:20 to soften the blow. That's the verse that says God can do immeasurably more than we can imagine. I didn't have the "other side" of the argument or the "What's in it for me?" All I had was Jesus saying, "Come and die." Dying to self means choosing to walk the narrow road of following Jesus.

As it says in Romans 12:1–2 (NIV), "Therefore, I urge you, brothers and sisters, in view of God's mercy, to offer your bodies as a living sacrifice, holy and pleasing to God—this is your true and proper worship." As believers of Jesus, followers of Jesus, and children of God, because of the vast, limitless mercy of God lavished upon our lives, gratitude should drive our hearts to give the fullness of our lives to Him as a joyful, set-apart offering. This is the purest way we can honor, love, and worship Him! I appreciate the way Peterson phrases this passage in his paraphrase of the Bible, *The Message*: *"So here's what I want you to do, God helping you: Take your everyday, ordinary life—your sleeping, eating, going-to-work, and walking-around life—and place it before God as an offering. Embracing what God does for you is the best thing you can do for Him."*

It's in the dying of self that embracing God's design and desires for our life begins. It's also in the dying of self that we begin living in the culture of God's Kingdom, which is where I believe true faith and monumental life are realized. In every way, this was where I had to willingly give up living for appearances, acceptance, and applause. The dying and denial of self is where pulseless religion bows to personal relationship with Jesus—and where the flesh comes to a reckoning, fully submitting and enabling a life of true resurrection power. As a wise friend once said, "Without death, there is no resurrection."

Though we try, there is simply no possible way to begin living and walking in the resurrection power of Jesus without first dying to self. This means there is also no possible way to live in God's callings, invitations, assignments, or good plans apart from first willingly laying our life on the altar as an offering.

Once God awakened me to this profound text, I realized this text and truth was authentic Christianity in its purest form—what Jesus not only desired but also invited and called us to. That said, can I confess to you honestly what an incredibly difficult command it is to obey, especially daily. It becomes much more challenging when this conviction starts to invade your personal goals, dreams, and desires.

I tend to be somewhat stubborn, often choosing the longest route to realize that without fully surrendering my own will, I can never fully embrace God's ways. The truth is that God's designs and desires are far greater than anything I could ever conceive for myself, but oh, how difficult it is to genuinely believe this! It's a hard truth, but this verse invites each of us to heed it.

An Invitation

Our God is supernatural and mysterious, and He desires to move in and through our lives; however, this can't fully happen as long as we hold on to our natural inclinations and motivations. Galatians 2:20 both awakens and incites us to the necessity of dying a willing, sacrificial, spiritual death to self, so we can become fully alive and filled with faith by the power of the Holy Spirit.

This really is the beginning of an abundant, significant, and monumental life! Jesus modeled it for us well. He willingly chose to become the last dead sacrifice on the cross so that we, in turn, could embrace our cross daily, to become His living sacrifices. Please hear me say this: I in no way claim to have spiritually arrived or become an expert at this calling. It's a day-by-day invitation, and I've been on this journey for nearly twenty-eight years, with some good days and some, well, let's just say praise Jesus for grace.

I know how my heart craves God's best for my life, but the journey must also involve patience, pace, and grace. Often, I find myself encouraged by guys in the Scriptures like Noah, whom God waited to use until the ripe age of six hundred, or Abraham, who (as far as we know) only began to walk into his monumental mission when he was around the age of seventy-five. There are also some troubled cases like Peter, Paul, or David. Who would have thought God could take such messy men and create such monumental messaging through their lives that would speak so profoundly down through the ages?

An Exhortation

Like the Hebrew term *zikrown*, our lives have the high and holy privilege of becoming mementos of God's miraculous power—monuments stacked together for maximum impact, created and built by God for His renown. I believe Peter understood the gravity of this invitation, which is why he exhorted Christ's followers in the way he did. In 1 Peter 2 (NLT), we see Peter open this part of his letter by unapologetically calling those under his care, along with future generations, to "get rid of all evil behavior. Be done with all deceit, hypocrisy, jealousy, and all unkind speech." He goes on to say, "Like newborn babies, you must crave pure spiritual milk so that you will grow into a full experience of salvation. Cry out for this nourishment now that you have tasted the Lord's kindness."

—

Our lives have the high and holy privilege of becoming mementos of God's miraculous power.

I hope you are picking up what Peter is putting down here, because his encouragement resonates loudly from generation to generation with the gravity of its truth. Peter implores us to pursue godliness and spiritual maturity, to put away the old life's attributes—dying to self, sin, past habits, or unholy hobbies. He calls us to be different, set apart, and holy.

To be sanctified means to be set apart. When God calls us and puts His hand upon our life, He also puts His holiness *in* our life. And while I am someone who greatly needs and deeply appreciates grace, I can't ignore Paul's indictment in Romans 6, which reminds us that to continue in sin is ridiculous in light of God's goodness! Of course, we receive grace, but it's that very grace that should bring a depth of gratitude for such a great salvation!

Paul and Peter's exhortations leave no excuse for trying to live a double life, part sacred and part secular. Romans 8 (NLT) says, "If the Spirit of Him who raised Jesus from the dead is living in us, He who raised Christ from the dead will give life to our mortal bodies because of His Spirit who lives in us." When we submit our lives to the authority of the Holy Spirit of God, holiness becomes the byproduct. I have found that when I struggle with holiness, the culprit is usually a lack of submission and surrender in some aspect of my life.

—

When God calls us and puts His hand upon our life, He also puts His holiness in our life.

Can I submit to you that the assignments and callings of God are not only irrevocable, according to Romans 11:29, but also too great for us, resulting in the total necessity of and dependence upon God? That means we don't have the luxury of trying to live with a foot in each world. Our mission requires surrender, accompanied by the Holy Spirit's activity in our lives! Peter knew that our submission is never contingent upon our ability or self-discipline, no matter how strong we may think we are.

Still, a life of submission and surrender should come with a deeper appreciation and gratitude for God's kindness, which consistently calls us to repentance, intimacy, and Christlikeness. I believe this is why Peter said this in 1 Peter 2:2–3 (NLT): "Cry out for this nourishment now that you have tasted the Lord's kindness." It's in the crying out that we find His nearness, and it's in His kindness that we become more Christlike.

The Journey of the Monumental Life

I have a spiritual father named Allen Tarbutton. He and his wife, Doris, have been unwavering pillars of faith in Kelly's and my life. They've often reminded us that "the journey is too great for us." We've felt this truth at different points in our lives, whether through loss, sickness, financial struggles, or facing relational pain due to the loss of friends along the way, mainly as a result of decisions we've made in faith. Their encouragement comes from a story in 1 Kings 19, when Elijah found himself in a precarious and challenging situation.

—

Dying to self is the tearing down of undeserving altars built to lesser gods in our lives.

The great prophet had just witnessed God's miraculous movement and supernatural intervention, and now he was strangely running for his life due to a threat. We'll come back to that later, but know this: Elijah had rebuilt an altar to the Lord after tearing down the unworthy altars from the cult followers of Baal and embarrassing them and their false gods in grand fashion. That's what dying to self is, in a significant way. It's the tearing down of undeserving altars built to lesser gods in our lives, so we can fully surrender to and build the proper altar to the one true, deserving God.

Recognizing the greatness of God and being humbled by the kindness of God invites us to deeper levels of gratitude and appreciation of God. This is the God who created the cosmos yet remains intimately and intentionally interested and invested in our lives. That fact should inspire new depths of desire to trust and follow Him, regardless of the circumstances. That knowledge should also be so compelling that it drives our worship of Him and our hunger for personal holiness unto Him. I believe Elijah had an innate understanding of this journey, and I have to think that Peter considered it too when imploring us to pursue spiritual depth and maturity.

It's as if Peter knew that once we understand that the sovereign, set apart, all-powerful God passionately loves us, it becomes impossible to desire or give our affections to anyone or anything else. How incredible that the God of Abraham, Moses, Peter, and Elijah desires to partner with us! He is the same God who parted the waters to make a way for His people where there was no way, and now He is calling us to great things and giving us assignments that demand a depth of dependency and faith in Him. What an amazing and humbling privilege!

Living Stones Rather Than Tombstones

I think it was Pastor Greg Laurie who once warned against having a saved soul, but living a wasted life. How tragic it would be to live your whole existence for nothing more than comfort, pleasure, applause, fame, or affluence—all of which, apart from Christ, reap nothing but emptiness, darkness, and death. We can choose to do it our way, which will lead only to a tombstone that represents an easily forgotten life, or we can choose to live according to God's intention for our lives, which will make us living stones. The real legacy is in the living stones.

In chapter 2 of his letter, Peter goes on to say, "You are coming to Christ, who is the living cornerstone of God's temple. He was rejected by people, but God chose him for great honor. And you are living stones that God is building into his spiritual temple. What's more, you are His holy priests. Through the mediation of Jesus Christ, you offer spiritual sacrifices that please God." (NLT)

These are powerful truths that Peter declared over us, the church. Jesus, being the living foundation of it all, and rightly the focus, was rejected by many but chosen by God for great honor. As a result, we too can expect the same type of treatment. While we can delight in the honor of being chosen by God, we can also expect to face challenges from people, as Jesus did. I have come to believe that this is an unfortunate attribute of saying yes to God's assignments. As I alluded to earlier, I've lost some of my closest friends and felt the sting of rejection more times than I care to recall out of obedience to God. I've also allowed this to become personally debilitating at times. I know too well and have choked down the bitter pill of pain as part of the process, but I believe it to be an expected part of the path when following Jesus. Not everyone will understand or embrace God's desires and designs for your life as you do; therefore, we must learn to differentiate between

The real legacy is in the living stones.

misalignment and being misunderstood. We cannot allow things like loss of relationships or rejection to define us or derail us from God's created destiny for our lives! We must come to a place where the approval and acceptance of God matters far more than the applause of men.

We must come to a place where the approval and acceptance of God matters far more than the applause of men.

It's a life-giving truth that Peter declared over those who choose to follow Jesus: We are considered "living stones" that God is using to build His spiritual house. Think about this: We are all "living stones," the "mementos and monuments" that God is using to build a memorial of remembrance for His glory! Peter is saying that God desires to use our lives to be the living *zikrown*, pillars, those living mementos who, unified together, declare the truth of our miraculous God to the world.

When you look at it this way, it becomes even more desirable to die to this empty and unsatisfying world, to be fully fulfilled and made alive spiritually, as a living monument to His Name. Peter then calls us "priests" who minister to God through spiritual sacrifices, because of Jesus's claim over our lives. This is what is pleasing to God. It's not so much our ability, talent, or "works" that please God, in and of themselves; it's more so the blood of Jesus covering us and calling us into a redeemed, holy, and intimate relationship with Him that instructs our offerings and is pleasing to Him.

There also seems to be corporate language in Peter's exhortations. It's as if, while there is absolutely a personal component to what Peter is saying, there's a greater sense of God doing something with us, incarnate, as a collective. It's the story-within-a-greater-story approach. God desires to use our lives personally in great measure—but also in even greater measure together, when unified corporately. We are the "living stones" of His greater story.

Let me illustrate this for you.

The Bethany Bunch

There was a family that was incredibly close to Jesus, one that Jesus loved and used in profound ways. The siblings were named Mary, Martha, and Lazarus, and they lived in a town called Bethany. Their story plays out in John 11 and 12.

Each person in this family had a significant story to tell throughout their life, and each person's testimony planted a seed that provided a harvest for generations to come. Each person's life became a living stone, a memento (*zikrown*), important on its own—but even more powerful in the context of the whole.

Lazarus experienced true resurrection power after Jesus called him back to life. Martha responded to Jesus's Lordship with service and hospitality, but it was Mary who longed to bask in His presence. She chose what was best by sitting at the feet of Jesus in adoration while hanging on to every word He spoke and every moment she could have with Him.

In John's gospel account, it's six days before Passover, the day when Jesus would triumphantly enter Jerusalem for the last time. There is a dinner at Lazarus's house to celebrate his resurrection, but more importantly, to honor Jesus. Lazarus is reclining at the table with Jesus as Martha serves, but Mary, in my imagination, is desperately trying to find a way to express her love and gratitude to Jesus. Finally, she decides to bring her most prized possession to Him as an offering. We see her take an incredibly expensive bottle of perfume, made from oil of nard and valued at the equivalent of three hundred full-day wages, and pour it over Jesus's feet. This is a lavish gift and offering. Self-righteous and sinister, Judas condemns this action as wasteful. If Mary wanted to do something of real meaning with her valuable offering, he suggests, why not sell it and take care of the poor? This is nothing more than impious, religious posturing on the part of Judas. Not only that, but if Judas had been allowed to steward that transaction, surely he would have sifted some of the proceeds into his own pocket, as he had been doing all along.

Mary still hadn't finished. She then took down her hair—a significant act in her culture, where a woman's hair was considered her crown or glory. Mary then proceeded to wipe Jesus's feet with her hair, which she had anointed with the expensive perfume.

Do you see it? Mary, the one who loved to sit transfixed at the feet of Jesus while Martha served feverishly, chose to honor Jesus with great humility, extravagance, and sacrifice. The Scripture says that the whole house was filled with the fragrance. Many read that and assume the fragrance that filled the house was from the perfume, but I think that the house was filled with the fragrance of Mary's worship. After all, what powerful imagery of an intimate heart for Jesus: She revered His glory so much that she lavished Him with such extravagance, only to wipe His feet with what was considered her glory.

In response to Judas's judgment and admonishment, Jesus offered His own rebuke: "Leave her alone. She did this in preparation for my burial." Again, we see a story within a story. Even Mary, at this moment, is being used for something monumental that will be remembered and discussed for all time.

In Mark's gospel, we find a story strikingly similar to this one. Theologians have long debated if these are accounts of the same story, with differing recollections of the details. Or they may be completely different events that just happen to be incredibly similar.

Either way, rather than taking place in Lazarus's house in Bethany, Mark's account takes place at the house of Simon, who was a man Jesus had previously healed of leprosy. Here, it is two days before Passover and the Festival of Unleavened Bread. According to Mark's tale, in chapter 14 in the NLT, a woman comes in with a beautiful alabaster jar of perfume, opens it, and pours it over Jesus's head.

Like Judas, the Scripture says that some at the table, seeing this take place, became indignant and expressed the same sentiments made by Judas in John's account. However, this time, Jesus gives a stronger rebuke. We see it in verses 6-9:

"Leave her alone. Why criticize her for doing such a good thing to me? You will always have the poor among you, and you can help them whenever you want to. But you will not always have me. She has done what she could and has anointed my body for burial ahead of time. I tell you the truth, wherever the Good News is preached throughout the world, this woman's deed will be remembered and discussed."

Do you see what Jesus just said? His rebuke included an incredible and prophetic reality: "Wherever the gospel will be declared throughout *the world*, the offering of this woman will be remembered!"

The woman Jesus speaks of marked that moment with a sacrifice that would be memorialized from that point forward. The legacy of her loving deed would forever be remembered and discussed, a step of faith unto the Lord. Mary's life still speaks as we discuss her offering and obedience to this day.

Every Step & Seed Is Significant

Consider this: Every act of worship, every step of faith, every stone of remembrance stacked, every seed planted, every love-inspired, faithful deed dedicated unto the Lord will be memorialized and remembered from here on out. Every moment of every day presents new opportunities to be an offering to God.

Whether the legacy we leave causes future generations to remember and discuss or only heaven applauds our offerings, the life we live unto the Lord greatly matters! Our choices to walk in faith and obedience build a monument to His Name for His glory.

Our choices to walk in faith and obedience build a monument to His Name for His glory.

Each day presents us with opportunities for such worship-driven faith and obedience. When we choose, like Mary, the better thing—living life for the adoration of Jesus—then everything we do can become an offering of praise.

There's a song that has gripped me of late. It's called "Center," written by Brian Johnson with Gabriel and Abbie Gamboa. There's one specific lyric that arrested my heart the first time I heard it, and it has quickly become the cry of my existence:

My whole life for Your glory, my whole world for You only,

Everything for the honor of Your Name.

If my days tell a story, let it be of You only,

Everything for the honor of Your Name.

Jesus, I love You!

Even typing the lyrics evokes an immediate emotional response. Any time that song is sung in worship, I am moved to tears because it captures the deepest desire and longing of my heart. I say that with a sense of reckless honesty, while still knowing, in the dark caverns in my soul, that I struggle to live in submission and surrender. I'm fully aware of my propensity to shift blame like Adam, deceive like Jacob, get angry like Moses, feel paranoid and depressed like Saul, hide and cover things up like David, run like Peter, and doubt like Thomas. Truth be told, if you are anything like me, we are all a bunch of screwed-up, misfit, unreliable, disqualified instruments that, for some reason, God sees fit to restore, redeem, and make His monuments.

—

Truth be told, if you are anything like me, we are all a bunch of screwed-up, misfit, unreliable, disqualified instruments that, for some reason, God sees fit to restore, redeem, and make His monuments.

Even the many legends of faith we read about in Scripture were seemingly flawed and imperfect. Still, God, in His kindness, took the broken pieces—the stones of their stories—and built something beautiful, powerful, and deeply meaningful. I believe Peter must've had this in mind when he talked about our being "*living stones* that God is building into His spiritual temple." Peter, of all people, knew the depth of his own sin but didn't allow it to define him.

If you want to see a master class in denial, look no further. At one point, Peter denied knowing Jesus in order to save himself, but in His kindness, Jesus chose to forgive and restore him so that Peter could finally fully surrender his life to Jesus. What could have just as easily and rightly been a tombstone, Jesus made into a living stone.

Yes, many of the mothers and fathers of faith we read about in the Bible were tragically flawed and deeply sinful. This is why the gospel is such good news. Even though while we were still deep in our darkness, debauchery, struggle, and sin, Christ chose to die for us. Not only did He demonstrate His unflinching and unwavering love for us in this way, He also declared His unconditional plan to redeem us.

If, like me, you've ever felt unqualified, disqualified, like a frequent flyer on the struggle bus, or stuck in a sinful pattern, be encouraged today. Know that you are not alone, and you are also in good company. You can't outrun or out-sin the grace of God. He's more powerful than you. Ask Mary Magdalene, ask Paul, ask Moses, ask me. Also, you won't be able to ignore or undo the invitations and callings of God. Ask Peter, ask David, ask Elijah. He's relentless in His pursuit, and passionate in His purpose, which makes me incredibly thankful. No matter how far I've ever run, or how much I've messed up in my life, my deepest hope is that I will live my life for His glory and worthy of His Name, His presence, and His calling—*because* of His greatness and goodness.

You can't outrun or out-sin the grace of God. He's more powerful than you. Ask Mary Magdalene, ask Paul, ask Moses, ask me.

Significance Begins at Surrender

As we close this chapter, let me circle back by way of encouragement. Every day that God awakens us and puts breath in our lungs, it's for a significant reason. The monumental life doesn't just happen. While I am so thankful for and believe in the unconditional grace of God, I also believe that faith without works is dead.

Every day, we have a choice to make about whether we will deny ourselves so that we may walk rightly with God. Every day we have a choice to make about whether to walk in boldness of faith. Sometimes, we have a choice to make about whether we will choose the less-traveled narrow road or the three C's of compromise, comfort, and convenience. Each and every day presents opportunities to worship God through our choices, actions, words, and deeds. Whatever we do, the daily choices we make either contribute to the building of a monument to His Name for His glory—or the opposite.

To be the living stones of that monument, we must begin by dying to self, no matter the cost. We must choose to surrender, day by day. Again, as Peterson so eloquently paraphrased the first two verses of Romans 12, we have the invitation to *"take our everyday, ordinary life—our sleeping, eating, going-to-work, and walking-around life—and place it before God as an offering."*

It's a humbling reality that we have this God-designed opportunity to offer our lives, both personally and collectively, as living stones being built by God into a spiritual temple that hosts His presence and brings Him honor.

Pray this prayer with me:

Father, I thank You for Your grace, Your forgiveness, and Your faithfulness in pursuing me. Jesus, would You arrest my heart for the glory and honor of Your Name? May I be a living stone, dead to self and fully made alive in You. Fill me with Your Holy Spirit today, I pray, and empower me to walk in irresistible hospitality like Martha, deep affection and honor like Mary, resurrected power like Lazarus, and spiritual maturity like Peter. Father, I thank You that no matter what I've done, it's nothing You can't redeem. Help me be that living stone, a memento of remembrance, pointing to and declaring the greatness of Your Name! Build Your monument in and through my life, I pray. There is no greater honor, nor anything worth more in life, than this. And Jesus, "If my days tell a story, let it be of You only, everything for the honor of Your Name.

Jesus, I love You!" Amen.

08

IT'LL ALL BE WORTH IT

ACTS 20:24 (NLT)

What matters most to me is to finish what God started:
the job the Master Jesus gave me of letting everyone I meet
know all about this incredibly
extravagant generosity of God.

A Monument Worth Living For

Over my years in ministry, I've walked with countless families through dark nights of the soul, particularly as they've navigated great hardship or loss. In the process, I've noticed a consistent pattern of two different responses people have when they lose a loved one. One response involves grief, but with a sense of gratitude and a feeling of grace-filled, peaceful release. I've seen it time and time again. For these people, there's a merciful comfort in the God who gives and takes away. No matter the hardship, it seems these people have a hope-based capacity to say, "Nevertheless, blessed be the Name of the Lord," as paraphrased from Job 1:21.

The other response I've witnessed is often a chaotic mix of crippling hopelessness and deep regret. This type of response, if not dealt with properly, can lead to an incapacitated life of anger, bitterness, and deep feelings of everything being senseless. In my own experiences with hardship and grief, I can assure you that, even amid trials and loss, God is always at work and can build something monumental in your life. When you walk with Jesus in faith, no matter the cost, it will all be unfathomably worth it in the end.

When you walk with Jesus in faith, no matter the cost, it will all be unfathomably worth it in the end.

Because of this, I encourage you to embrace each day and every moment as an opportunity to stack those stones of remembrance, plant those seeds of faith, and continue to take the necessary steps to ensure a life and legacy that align with God's purposes and desires. We must realize that if we aren't living a life that builds a monument to God, then we are assuredly building one to something or someone else.

In Luke 11, Jesus says we are either gatherers or scatterers. Either we are working with God or against Him. In James, it states that we are either friends of God or enemies. We are living our lives as either missionaries or in a mission field. And, as it says in Matthew 6:24, no one can serve two masters. Again, our greatest challenge is to ensure that we aren't *leaning the ladder of our lives against the wrong wall.* We don't want to run the race of our lives building undeserving altars to lesser gods, whether accolades, achievement, affluence, or the applause of men. None of these things could ever truly build a monumental life. It's not that you can't make an impact in these ways; it's just that the impact won't stand the test of eternity.

I've heard it said that we will encounter two moments of judgment when standing before a holy God. First, what did you decide for your life about following Jesus? Second, what did you do with your life *because* you followed Jesus? What if we chose to live each day like it was our last, or as the great accidental theologian Tim McGraw put it, we "lived like we're dying"? Quite frankly, we are! We don't have as much time as we think we do, and far too much is at stake.

When we leave this life and our faith becomes sight, I guarantee we won't be thinking about the wealth we accumulated or the number of followers we attracted. No, all we will care about is what we hear when standing before the King, our Creator. That moment will be the single most important conversation of the totality of our existence. What an honor and privilege to spend the rest of our days preparing for that encounter! Not only that, but how incredible it is to have the knowledge and promise that our God desires to walk with us, work in us and through us, provide everything we need, and be with us every step of the way.

If we aren't living a life that builds a monument to God, then we are assuredly building one to something or someone else.

As I described in chapter 5, my greatest hope in this life is to honor the Lord and walk with Him in such radical faith that one day I look back in wonder and amazement at where I find myself. That's been my dream and my wife's dream since we launched into our life together. We've already accepted that the journey, at times, will be too hard or great for us, which makes us wholly dependent upon God.

With that said, I'd like to propose that if the dream, vision, or promise you're embarking on is something you can handle on your own, maybe it's not God's full calling for your life. Over the years, I've become increasingly convinced that God's plans, purposes, and promises are always bigger than I can imagine or accomplish on my own. If the vision, dream, or promise is too big for you, then you've probably, in faith, moved into God's zip code. This has proven to be true time and again in my own life, as evidenced by our student conference called 220. Had you told me twenty-five years ago,

If the vision, dream, or promise is too big for you, then you've probably, in faith, moved into God's zip code.

when we launched 220, what it would look like today, I never would have believed you. I can also say that had you told me the holistic cost, I'm not sure I would have had the fortitude or faith to fully engage God's design, embrace His desires, and endure. Humbly, I'm thankful God didn't give me all the information at the point of His invitation, because now I can say I've had the joy of learning that if the sacrifice, service, or assignment goes beyond you, then you're in good company with the many faith fathers and mothers we read about in Scripture. Truth be told, I wouldn't trade any moment of these last twenty-five years as part of this ministry. It's been overwhelming at times—but also overwhelmingly worth it.

—

It's the God factor that transforms the ordinary and unlikely into the extraordinary and profound.

Consider all the people we've studied throughout our lives who received a promise from the Lord with an assignment attached. Again, I can't help but think about Abraham. I also consider the improbable shepherd boy named David, who would become a king. Then there are the other unlikely figures: Mary, the young teenage virgin mother of Jesus; Rahab, a prostitute turned providential who was willing to risk it all for God's people; and let's not forget Moses, whose story was as complex as a soap opera. Yes, God's promises and assignments seem to find the most unlikely and ordinary people, people whose lives eventually unfold into glorious monuments declaring God's faithfulness and greatness!

It's the God factor that transforms the ordinary and unlikely into the extraordinary and profound. Such are the personal stories in Scripture of those who point to an even greater story about Him! Every story is a shrine unto the Lord, and every shrine is built on a series of small, faithful steps over a long period of time in the same direction. Every step of obedience, taken in faith, is a stone stacked to form a monument unto His great Name.

We Have to See It in Faith

What about us? Yes, the journey will be too great for us alone. The promise, vision, and assignment of God may even ask us to plant seeds for trees we never see with our own eyes. But make no mistake: Harvest will come.

I'm reminded once again of Elijah at the Mount Carmel showdown. We find the drama unfolding in 1 Kings 18 (NLT). The point of the story is simple: The Lord God of Israel in Scripture is the one true God, full stop. Elijah found himself in a position to prove this in stunning fashion. In his story, we see the faith steps and the seeds planted, but we also see a daring and dramatic display put to the test.

It begins with God sending Elijah to prophesy a drought. The kingdom of Israel was divided into two parts at the time, one of which was under the rule of a king named Ahab, along with his manipulative wife, Jezebel. Jezebel not only chose to worship false gods but also put a death sentence on the prophets of the one true God. Months would go by, crops would die, streams and rivers would dry up, and people would suffer. God did not desire that people suffer needlessly, but He did desire to get their attention and bring them into alignment. I've found that often God may allow our circumstances to shift, to shake us and get our attention. The culmination of this duel would be an emphatic and epic scriptural showdown.

The promise, vision, and assignment of God may even ask us to plant seeds for trees we never see with our own eyes. But make no mistake: Harvest will come.

When finally meeting in confrontation, Elijah would inform Ahab that it wasn't he, Elijah, who was the issue—rather, it was indeed the king and his wife. It's then that Elijah challenged the king and his depraved wife to gather 450 prophets of the god Baal, and 400 prophets of the god Asherah, all of whom, according to 1 Kings 18:16–19 (NLT), "*Eat at Jezebel's table.*" In other words, Queen Jezebel was a wicked woman who kept evil company, and the prophet Elijah wasn't having it.

Here is where things got interesting.

The Battle

Elijah issued his challenge, likely to everyone's amazement, as well as to everyone's agreement. He created a scenario where it appeared that he would be alone against all 450 prophets of Baal—all the priests of the false gods versus one who worshipped the true God. Now was the time for people to decide: If God was the one true God, they should follow Him; but if Baal was the one true god, then they should follow him. What would it be?

Elijah set it up perfectly because of his immovable faith and confidence in the one true God. He allowed them to choose first from the bulls. He then allowed them to prepare the bulls and the altar, and to call upon *their god* to receive the sacrifice on their altar. They did so, to no avail.

He taunted them, saying, "Shout louder! I'm sure Baal is a god! Perhaps he has too much to think about. Or maybe he has gone to the toilet. Or perhaps he's away on a trip. Maybe he's sleeping. You might have to wake him up."

There would be no reply, even after the priests danced, shouted, and cut themselves, which is typical in occult activity. At this point, I imagine Elijah quietly and methodically began to rebuild the once-ravaged altar to the Lord. He took twelve stones, which represented the twelve tribes of Israel, and placed firewood upon them. He then dug a ditch (or a moat) around the altar. At this point, he placed a bull on top of the wood. How appropriate that the stones, which represented God's people, would hold the offering before the Lord.

Here's where the story moves from incredible to supernatural.

Elijah asked people to soak the altar, which was to be consumed by fire, with water from four large containers, all to prove that the one true God is indeed all-powerful. Please don't miss this. Take stock of what Elijah asked them to do—and during a drought, mind you! One soaking wouldn't be enough. Elijah wanted to ensure that the people in attendance would thoroughly understand the message, so he asked them to repeat the action not once, not twice, but three times. During a drought, Elijah commanded them to soak the altar with the precious commodity of water until it was completely saturated.

Elijah wanted to ensure that no question would remain regarding the power of the one true God. When it came time for evening sacrifice, Elijah stepped forward. He prayed this way in 1 Kings 18:36–37 (NIRV):

"Lord, You are the God of Abraham, Isaac, and Israel. Today, let everyone know that You are God in Israel. Let them know I'm Your servant. Let them know I've done all of these things because You commanded me to. Answer me, Lord, answer me. Then these people will know that You are the one and only God. They'll know that You are turning their hearts back to You again."

It was then that it happened: The Lord sent fire, completely consuming the offering. The fire consumed not only the bull and the wood, but also the stones, soil, and the water in the ditch. There is no possible way that ordinary fire could consume dirt, rocks, and water, but that is precisely what happened. Surely, this was no ordinary God!

Everyone who witnessed this supernatural act of omnipotent power on display acknowledged the one true God, who then sent Elijah to put all the false prophets to death. As this story involving Elijah made the emphatic point that the Lord God is the one, true, and actual God, the Lord God is also the point and purpose of *our* lives, and we are invited to live as a declaration of this truth.

Our Epic Battle

We have our own fight to deal with, an epic battle of dying to self and daily denying self. To sum it up simply: Our lives, day by day, are an epic spiritual duel, much like the story of Elijah, Ahab, and Jezebel. Each day, we will encounter the false gods of this world and have choices to make about whether to walk intimately with the one true God or hand in hand with undeserving idols. Each day, we must decide whether to carry our cross and walk in the ways of Jesus or to cave in and compromise, capitulating to the culture of this world.

Make no mistake: We have an enemy whose whole desire is to steal from us, kill us, and do all he can to destroy us before we can step into God's destiny for our lives. The last thing he wants us to understand and live is our God-created identity. The enemy knows that if we begin to realize who we are to God—as Abraham, Moses, Jacob, and Elijah did—then we will become incredibly dangerous to his plan. When we begin to understand whom we belong to, who we are in Christ, what we possess in Him, and what He calls us to, then there is no Jericho, no giant, no mountain, and no minion of the devil that can keep us from fully living all God has in mind for us.

We need more daring saints who are willing to risk it all.

Understanding our identity in Christ sets us up for greater displays of God's power, glory, and goodness than what even Elijah witnessed. We need more daring saints who are willing to risk it all because their trust and faith are so secure in who God is, as well as what God can and will do.

Will that be you?

Will your testimony declare God's ability to overcome any obstacle, break any and every chain, move any mountain, tear down any wall, and make a way, time and time again, where there seems to be no way?

Will your faith enable you to see the clouds, hear the rain, and build the boat, even under clear blue skies?

Will you be faithful to prophesy God's provision and take steps of faith, even when God doesn't give you the coordinates or the plan?

Will you remain steadfast in seasons of hardship and pain?

What about in the midst of hardship, trial, and those dark nights of the soul—will you still stand and say, "Blessed be Your Name," believing it all to be worth it in every way?

Will every detail of your life be given to the Lord as His monument, standing as a reminder for the generations that will come after you of the power and providential goodness, faithfulness, and greatness of God?

What Do You Hear God Saying?

As the faith-filled miracle moment on Mount Carmel concluded, Elijah exercised his prophetic assignment by declaring yet another awe-inspiring miracle to come. Rather than fire, this time, much-needed rain would fall. Elijah said to Ahab, *"Go get something to eat and drink, for I hear a mighty rainstorm coming!"*

Regardless of how ludicrous it may have sounded, this had to be an incredible thing to hear after three years of drought, which represented a sense of barren dryness and need—but at this point, who was Ahab to question Elijah after all he had just witnessed? Now, after a supernatural display of God's reality on Mount Carmel, Elijah said he saw a cloud in the Spirit and prophesied rain!

Elijah then climbed to the top of the same mountain where God had just sent down fire, bowed low in reverence, and waited to hear from the Lord. After spending some time in prayer, Elijah called for his servant and sent him seven times to look at the skies out toward the sea, searching for a cloud or any evidence of rain.

Elijah firmly believed, in faith, what was to come based solely on what God had revealed to him. It was the seventh time that his servant finally returned and said, *"I saw a little cloud about the size of a man's hand rising from the sea."* That was all Elijah needed to hear, because he now knew that the time was at hand.

Let this encourage you. When God says it, we can believe we will see it. The opportunity before us is to believe what we see in the Spirit, before we see anything with our eyes. It's not that our faith makes things come to fruition; it's that our faith allows us to believe God! Because of who God is, we can believe we will see what He says we will see. As Scripture says in Hebrews 11:1 (ESV), faith is *"the assurance of things hoped for, and the conviction of things not seen."* Also, simply by nature of who God is, we can know beyond any shadow of doubt that anything God invites us to will be worth it, by every measure. Elijah was so sure of God and what God had said that he believed with absolute conviction in his spirit that God would do it, even if he wasn't seeing it with his eyes just yet.

—

It's not that our faith makes things come to fruition; it's that our faith allows us to believe God!

Such is the monumental life God is calling us to.

Such is your God-given vision, and such is the dream God has for your life!

Like Elijah, we must see and believe in faith what will come, based solely on what we hear God saying. We know in His word that He gives us certain promises. For example, in John 10 (NLT), Jesus says: "My purpose is to give them a rich and satisfying life."

Ephesians 2:10 (NLT) says: "We are God's masterpiece. He has created us anew in Christ Jesus, so we can do the good things he planned for us long ago."

Romans 8:28 (NLT) says: "We know that God causes everything to work together for the good of those who love God and are called according to his purpose for them." And we also know He is unwaveringly faithful.

Psalm 33:11 (NIV) says: "The plans of the Lord stand firm forever, the purposes of His heart through generations."

God knows the plans that He has for us. His plans are good, and His plans include our peace and prosperity. His plans are full of hope for a bright future. As you know, this does not mean we won't encounter hardship, pain, loss, sifting, struggle, sorrow, sickness, or suffering, which are all products of the fall. This simply means that, no matter what our enemy intends for evil, God can and will turn it for our good. God will work it out, and it will be worth it. We can also trust that our God is always with us, and He will make a way where there seems to be no way.

Consider the Red Sea.

Consider the Jordan River.

Personally, I learned that through situations like the birth stories of both of my boys Jack and Kyle. When the barrier seems impassible or impossible, God's power and provision will always make His promises inevitable. This is the God who can make a way in the wilderness and streams in the wasteland, according to Isaiah 43. This is the God who can restore the years that the swarming locusts have eaten, according to Joel 2.

As it pertains to this monumental life that God has designed for you: You can believe it in faith, see it in the Spirit, and begin to move forward, taking those steps of faith, because it is the God of all creation who has dreamed it and said it. Remember, it was after a three-year drought, and an incredible display of the power of God, that Elijah sent word to Ahab that rain was coming. And it did, according to 1 Kings 18:45 (NLT): *"Black clouds filled the sky. The wind came up and heavy rains began to fall."*

—

When the barrier seems impassible or impossible, God's power and provision will always make His promises inevitable.

The people were surely exhilarated and refreshed. With all the events that had occurred, whom do you think they credited, as they danced in joy while the rain soaked the thirsty ground and replenished their parched souls? Like Elijah, may we be so passionate and so trusting of God that even when it seems He is silent, we continue to wait and see what He will say and do next. Because who knows? On the seventh try, we may begin to see that small cloud rise up and begin to swell.

When God Speaks in Our Sleep

Dreams are real, and God sometimes speaks to us through them—and not just the dreams of our hearts. There are times when God chooses to interrupt me in my sleep to speak to me, perhaps because it's quality time, when I'm still and quiet enough to listen. Whatever the case, God has made it His habit to partially awaken me during the night to give me things to write down. I've learned to listen and lean in, even if countless nights of tossing and turning have led me to that revelation.

There's a story involving Jacob in Genesis 28. It wasn't long after his father Isaac had blessed him, giving him specific instructions, that Jacob found himself traveling toward Haran. In verse 11, around sundown, he sets up for the evening to camp, finds a nice stone to rest his head on, lies down, and falls asleep. I'm not quite sure why he thought a stone would be a good idea for a pillow, but stay with me because this whole "stone for a pillow" thing will take on significant meaning. In verses 12 through 15, Jacob's sleep is interrupted:

As he slept, he dreamed of a stairway that reached from the earth up to heaven. And he saw the angels of God going up and down the stairway. At the top of the stairway stood the LORD, and he said, "I am the LORD, the God of your grandfather Abraham, and the God of your father, Isaac. The ground you are lying on belongs to you. I am giving it to you and your descendants. Your descendants will be as numerous as the dust of the earth! They will spread out in all directions—to the west and the east, to the north and the south. And all the families of the earth will be blessed through you and your descendants. What's more, I am with you, and I will protect you wherever you go. One day, I will bring you back to this land. I will not leave you until I have finished giving you everything I have promised you." (NLT)

—

How many times in our journey has God been trying to get our attention, invite us into His supernatural assignment, reveal to us His glory and goodness, and we aren't even aware of it?

Isn't it just like God to speak in the silence, in the storms, sometimes in the darkness, and even at times through dreams? Upon awakening, Jacob says, "Surely the Lord is in this place, and I wasn't even aware of it."

What an incredible realization upon this physical and spiritual awakening!

How many times in our journey has God been trying to get our attention, invite us into His supernatural assignment, reveal to us His glory and goodness, and we aren't even aware of it? Jacob, through this dream, has an encounter with God that leaves him breathless, in reverence and wonder, exclaiming in verse 17: *"What an awesome place this is! It is none other than the house of God, the very gateway to heaven!" (NLT)*

Oh, to be like Jacob in this hour. What an amazing opportunity to have God visit in a dream, revealing His goodness and providing encouragement on the journey. I wonder if it would be easy for us to recognize and step in faith if God visited us in such a manner?

Memorialize the Moment

The dream was enough to move Jacob to get up early the next morning, take the stone he had rested his head on, and set it upright as a memorial pillar. It's similar to the time Samuel raised an Ebenezer to God, anointing it with oil and naming that moment and that place "Bethel," which means, "house of God." Jacob had met with God in that place, in that moment, and wanted to memorialize it. However, the memorial wasn't just the stone; it was his vow.

In that moment and at that place, Jacob made a vow to God:

"If God will indeed be with me and protect me on this journey, and if he will provide me with food and clothing, and if I return safely to my father's home, then the LORD will certainly be my God. And this memorial pillar I have set up will become a place for worshiping God, and I will present to God a tenth of everything he gives me." Genesis 28:20-22 (NLT)

Jacob was saying that because of God's goodness and faithfulness, he would gladly give his life to honor, worship, and walk in faith and obedience unto the Lord. He would hold nothing back, since God was obviously holding nothing from him. Jacob may not have realized it, but it wasn't the stone He anointed that was the monument. It was the living stone, a stone named Jacob, that God was anointing—that was the monument. At least, that is the monument God was genuinely interested in.

Same God, Same Invitation

What if we were to realize the truth in this story for ourselves? What if we went all in, because we realize that God has gone all in on our behalf through Jesus? Truly, our God is worthy of the fullness of our attention, affections, and allegiance, and everything He has planned for us and invites us to will be monumentally worth it! He not only has invited us and called us but also more than willingly provides for every detail of our destiny and promises to be with us each step of the way.

He said it to Abraham before us—and to Moses, and Jacob, and on and on. God has a holy habit of walking with His people and working through His people. Jesus has revealed again and again how faithful He is and always will be. His life is worthy of emulation, and Paul instructs us to be imitators of God. Jesus serves as a constant example for us in how to live a life of radical faith, honor, and obedience unto the Father, as well as how to love people passionately and serve them with irresistible hospitality.

—

It's the choice to take those small, seemingly insignificant steps in the same direction every day that can create a monument of legacy.

Now, like Abraham and Jacob, I believe God is calling us, inviting us into His assignments, and blessing us to be a blessing to the world. The word God gave to Jacob was the very word He gave to his grandfather, Abraham. The promise God made generations before is the same promise He held Himself to when speaking to Jacob. I believe it's the same promise that He speaks to us today. God wants to make our lives a monument to His great Name and a blessing to the world.

The life we live truly matters. The choices we make daily, all the steps we take in faith, matter. Every stone we stack in remembrance, and the totality of our existence, matters deeply and is building a lasting legacy. It's the choice to take those small, seemingly insignificant steps in the same direction every day that can create a monument of legacy. And that legacy, surrendered to and offered to God, will be worth it and will outlive us.

He Still Speaks

This truth is on display in Hebrews 11:4 (NLT), where Abel is unexpectedly mentioned. While his inclusion may seem insignificant or random, it serves as a powerful and intentional reminder.

Consider what is said of Abel: "It was by faith that Abel brought a more acceptable offering to God than Cain did. Abel's offering gave evidence that he was a righteous man, and God showed his approval of his gifts. Although Abel is long dead, he still speaks to us by his example of faith." Did you catch that last sentence? "Although Abel is long dead, he still speaks to us by his example of faith." This statement reaches back to Genesis 4, and here, near the end of the Bible in Hebrews, we read this significant declaration about Abel.

—

A life offered to the Lord with legacy in mind is worth whatever sacrifice and cost it may require.

"Although Abel is long dead, he still speaks."

It was Abel's offering that gave evidence of his righteousness, which mirrors Genesis 15:6, where Abraham "believed God, and it was credited to him as righteousness." [4] Please know that Abel didn't earn this righteousness because of the gift he offered; it was the faith behind the gift that made him right with God. Abel knew that any offering made to God wasn't out of obligation, but opportunity. God was pleased, not because of Abel's performance, but because of his posture. Although his young life was cut short due to the jealousy of his brother, Cain, he is credited here in what we refer to as *the Hall of Faith*. What is fascinating and motivating about Abel is that long after

[4] James Boice, "Romans: Living By Faith," 1988, https://core.ac.uk/download/483523044.pdf.

he was gone, the Bible says his life continued to speak, as it still does to this day. His life and legacy continue to tell a greater story, echoing the truth that righteousness isn't earned, but received by faith.

Abel's life and steps of faith may seem insignificant due to the brief nature of his story, yet they were anything but! He showed us what true worship looks like. Abel's offering involved sacrifice, as all true worship does. Abel's life and story still speak, reminding us that faith comes at a cost—but to him, it was an opportunity that seemed worthy of pursuit.

—

Our every step taken in obedience is an offering.

A life offered to the Lord with legacy in mind is worth whatever sacrifice and cost it may require, regardless of the process, path, pain, change, or challenge. Therefore, we should embrace every moment as significant to ensure that our legacy aligns with His purposes! The real and worthy monuments are the living stones who are daily devoted to pointing to the faithfulness, power, love, greatness, and goodness of God.

Let me conclude this chapter with the following passage from Hebrews 13:20–21, as paraphrased by Eugene Peterson in *The Message*:

May God, who puts all things together, makes all things whole, who made a lasting mark through the sacrifice of Jesus, the sacrifice of blood that sealed the eternal covenant, who led Jesus, our Great Shepherd, up and alive from the dead, now put you together, provide you with everything you need to please him, make us into what gives him most pleasure, by means of the sacrifice of Jesus, the Messiah. All glory to Jesus forever and always! Oh, yes, yes, yes.

May we live with legacy in mind, realizing that our every step taken in obedience is an offering, significant in that those steps of faith build a monument that will continue to speak long after we are gone. May our lives stand as powerful monuments dedicated to the glory of Jesus, and may we wholeheartedly recognize the profound worth of this pursuit.

Pray this prayer with me:

Jesus, may I perceive You as completely good, unwaveringly holy, and undeniably worthy of the entirety of my life. May my life be the tapestry in which You paint your self-portrait, that I may look like You, love like You, and live like You, as long as there is breath in my lungs. May the sole purpose of my existence be as a memorial, a monument, unto Your great Name! When others look upon me, may they see You, Jesus! May I live to simply tell Your story and Your story only, Jesus. I pray this in Your Name alone, as I live for Your Name alone.

You are worthy of it all. Amen.

09

STUCK & SPECTATING (DON'T DIE IN HARAN)

> 1 CORINTHIANS 15:58 (MSG)
>
> With all this going for us, my dear, dear friends, stand your ground. And don't hold back. Throw yourselves into the work of the Master, confident that nothing you do for him is a waste of time or effort.

A Word of Warning

With everything already said, let me offer you this piece of advice: *Don't get stuck. Don't settle.*

There's something significant in the Scriptures about the number seven. Genesis speaks of God creating the world in six days and resting on the seventh. The book of Revelation talks about the seven spirits before God's throne and the seven churches. Exodus 23 speaks of working the land for six years and resting it on the seventh. It was on the seventh time of scanning the skies that Elijah declared rain was finally on the way. There were seven deacons chosen by the apostles in Acts 6. There is talk of seven seals, seven bowls, seven trumpets, seven days of marching, forgiving seventy times seven, and a sevenfold promise to Israel.

Seven seems to permeate the Scriptures with profound messaging containing deep and often encouraging meaning. The number seven appears over seven hundred times throughout both the Old and New Testaments, so it seems to be important to God. Therefore, there must be some relevance in it for us. In Biblical numerology, the number seven represents completion, perfection, or divine wholeness.

Seven

"Maybe you need to find another church."

Those seven words were said to me at the young age of nineteen. At the time, they were painful yet strangely providential. I couldn't see it in real time, but looking back now, I can see how God used that statement, in that moment, to completely shift my trajectory and set me on a path toward my God-created destiny. However, at the moment, nothing about it felt good. It didn't make me feel whole—quite the opposite—but it certainly brought things to completion.

—

Make no mistake: The enemy will come against any move of God, and he will come quickly.

My time at that church was complete, as hard as it was to admit or reconcile. I felt heartbroken, due to all that the church, and the relationships forged through it, had meant to me. Most of my adolescence, the main years of my spiritual formation, took place in that church. I came to know Jesus personally and intimately, was called to ministry, and was embraced by and poured into by many great pastors and lay leaders there. The church was full of friends who were more like family to me.

I began to understand the power of the Holy Spirit in that church, not because He was a strong part of our theological framework or methodology, but because God began to move in powerful ways at one point. Strangely, that is also when everything began to unravel and come crashing down. Make no mistake: The enemy will come against any move of God, and he will come quickly. Therefore, any move of God must be humbly, carefully, and diligently stewarded at all costs.

Years before that church began growing exponentially, our pastor had an encounter with God that completely changed him. The evidence was in his ministry. Our church began to be a place where the presence of God was tangible, impacting lives, introducing people to Jesus, and helping them develop a passion for His glory. The pastor didn't flip the script or do anything blasphemous or extreme, like replacing the hymnals with a screen or anything like that, but he did host the presence of Jesus differently.

During that time, a few men in servant-leadership positions, who feared losing control, took a level of spiritual authority that they weren't called to walk in, and they willfully chose to shut down the movement of God. They did this through much dissension, which ultimately resulted in achieving the goal of removing our pastor.

The season that followed was nothing short of a hot mess, not for the weak in faith or the faint of heart. The church developed a revolving door of pastors. Church business meetings began to sound more like political debates full of preferential opinions, weak on Biblical conviction. Other ministers lost their jobs or left, and many of the parishioners were hurt deeply.

It got so bad that one of the youth pastors even received a death threat slid under his office door. I know—that's *crazy*, right? Yet it was real, and it's what we were dealing with. I didn't realize it then, but God was teaching me that the church is not void of spiritual assignments, both from the Lord and from the devil. Jesus Himself told His disciples that He had called each of them, but there was a devil among them. This makes it clear that any time there is a divine move of God, it may also be accompanied by a deviant move in the assembly as well.

Assignments in the Assembly

Jesus chose the Twelve, and Judas was one of them. Don't get me wrong, He loved Judas, washed the feet of Judas, and maintained an open door for him, even to the end. This was the position my dad took toward these men who caused such mischief. He loved, served, and held out hope that God would move upon their lives and prayerfully change their hearts.

My dad was a man of deep faith and integrity, so he led our family in the difficult calling to live as a remnant in waiting, praying for the restoration of the glory of God back into God's house. Therefore, we stuck it out as long as we could. By this point, we had gone through many pastors. No pastor would stay long, especially if the committee couldn't control them.

This is when it happened: "Maybe you need to find another church."

All my life, I had been taught that the Bible was true, cover to cover, and I believed it. I had stumbled upon some passages where Jesus had given authority over demons and diseases, and I wanted to know more. It was then, at a moment when I was trying to stay connected, believing we weren't called to men but God and His mission, that I went to "the pastor of the month" and asked him about it. I was hoping to get some sort of reasonable explanation. Demons and disease, deliverance or healing—these kinds of things weren't really talked about in that church.

Rather than some sort of encouraging explanation, or even an "I don't know," my questions were met with rejection: "Maybe you need to find another church." Those seven words would not only sting with a forceful and painful reverberation, but they would also take me twenty-one years to reconcile, release, and forgive.

Upon hearing those words, I did what many of us so easily do.

I built a monument and an altar to my pain.

Altars of Pain

When we construct undeserving altars, we're usually left with pillars memorializing our pain. They are often the result of decisions made in grief or anger and may be accompanied by some kind of oath or vow. That vow, in turn, is typically a response to an unhealed wound, a self-preserving way of reminding ourselves to never allow something like that to happen again.

I never wanted to feel the gravity of that rejection again, so I built a rock of remembrance, so to speak, and then I found myself stuck at that altar of grief and hurt. When we enshrine our pain, it can lead to deadly consequences, such as unforgiveness, bitterness, and callousness, to name a few. I've often heard it said that bitterness and unforgiveness are like drinking poison while hoping the other person dies. My monument of pain became my lens on the world, the filter I lived by, and eventually, quite honestly, a god I worshipped. Yes, you read that right. Anger, pain, and grief are real and unavoidable emotions, but they make for terrible gods.

I became so invested in my hurt that I traded away necessary community for self-preservation, isolation, and diminishment of every remaining relationship in my life, including my relationship with God. By saying no to the things and people of God, I was also saying no to God!

—

When we construct undeserving altars, we're usually left with pillars memorializing our pain.

My logic went something like this: *Why would I say yes to God and embrace a life of ministry if ministry looks like the church of my youth?* After hearing those seven incapacitating words from the pastor, feeling "uninvited" and like *I didn't belong there anymore*, there was now no way I wanted to step into what God had called me to do. So, I found myself stuck.

God has a funny way of moving mountains by allowing us to face giants. Little did I know that what seemed to be a true setback was actually a total setup. God had a plan; even something as painful as my perceived rejection wouldn't thwart that. Right around the time I completed my tenure at that church, although reeling, I began receiving invitations from a newer local student pastor who would become one of my best friends. I had no idea that saying yes to a free lunch invitation from a youth pastor named Tim would turn into him becoming one of my biggest champions.

That meeting was providential in that it led him to invite me to help at his church, which was a plant led by my former pastor who had been removed years prior. God had used that pastor in such powerful ways at the church I grew up in, and the word on the street was that He was doing it again through this new fellowship. Though I had wanted to visit that church for some time, my dad's wisdom wouldn't allow us to follow men, only God. So I hadn't yet been given permission to check it out. However, now, with my newfound situation and freedom, my dad blessed this transition, enabling me to step into a house where the presence and power of God were actively at work. It was liberating and life-giving, to say the least. It was also an open door to a myriad of opportunities for engaging in ministry, though my friend Tim started slowly with me. I would come to find that being in the right church, under the right leadership, would launch me in every way into much of the same ministry I am still involved in.

—

God can take our altars of pain and turn them into altars of praise.

Of course, there are a ton of stories associated with that. Still, the point is this: We all endure painful moments where we sometimes feel stuck, but no matter the giants we face, God can take our altars of pain and turn them into altars of praise—if we are willing to remain faithful and keep following Him in faith and obedience. Situations that seem dire, even impossible, are where we often see God do His best work.

Here's the coolest part of the story.

Fast-forward twenty-one years, to October 7, 2015. By then, I had been involved in ministry for years and loved it, but if I was honest, a part of me still didn't feel fully functional. However, that day, I found myself at a church-planting conference in California, thanks to the invitation of another pastor who had been spiritually investing in me. Again, it was October 7 (did you catch that number?) when God decided to begin bringing restoration to one of my deepest wounds. In His kindness, referring to the pastor who rejected me, He whispered, "What if he didn't know the answer?"

Seven words.

After hours—days, really—of pressing in and praying through that message, God lovingly enabled me to fully and finally release that pastor, that point in my life, and that pain, but first He lovingly and gracefully allowed me to face that giant. It's not that I don't still have the scar from that battle, but there was finally beauty out of the ashes for the first time in twenty-one years. I found a different level and understanding of grace and forgiveness, and for the first time in a long time, I felt fully free. My release from the pain enabled me to receive new excitement, power, and a fresh anointing for a coming assignment—one that would be too big for me and feel quite monumental.

A new joy awakened in me. As I could now see my past as a great teacher, God used the path I had walked as part of a process of preparation that was at long last leading me into His design, the calling that God had placed upon my life at fifteen years old.

If God's Not Done, Neither Is the Enemy

We spent a lot of time in the first four chapters discussing the potential pitfalls of taking possession of God's promise and walking in our God-created potential. Remember:

- Don't be shocked when the devil tries to sideline you, even by using things we deem good (e.g., things of God, people of God).
- Don't be willing to settle for anything less than all God has for you.
- Don't get stuck, focused on the storm, suffering, sickness, or sifting.

God doesn't want us to be stuck or still in front of a monument to our pain. Don't get me wrong; there are moments, seasons, and situations where God commands us to "be still and know that He is God" (Psalm 46:10 NIV). However, by and large, I've found that those moments of stillness are for remembrance and worship. It's in the *selah* (the pause) where we recognize the source of true life and get what we need from Jesus. God deserves the fullness of our attention, which is why we pause for perspective, get still to see and speak of His worth, and wait in worship. However, He also desires us to be active and moving forward in faith and obedience, as illustrated many times over in Scripture:

- "Noah, though it may seem crazy, build a boat. Get to work! You'll need it to survive the storm that's coming."
- "Abram, take a step of faith with me. If you do, I'll bless the world through you."
- "Moses, lead My people toward My promise. I know you feel like it's complicated and that you are incapable."
- "Elijah, what are you doing hiding in the woods after what you've just witnessed? Get out of that cave and get busy being the person I've called you to be."

Jesus did tell His disciples to wait in Jerusalem for the promise, but then, almost in the same breath, He gave them a vision for multiplication and expansion beyond their wildest expectations or thoughts. It's not that Jesus wanted them to stay and settle. He wanted them to wait for what they needed before going forward in faith.

Hurry Up & Wait (It's Worth It)

Jesus's disciples were focused only on Jerusalem, but as Jesus said in Acts 1, "Wait here for a moment until the gift of the Holy Spirit comes and empowers you. Then, I am calling, commanding, and commissioning you to go to Jerusalem, Judea, Samaria, and the ends of the earth." (NIV)

Jesus had an assignment for His disciples, a life and purpose far greater than what they imagined for themselves. Far too often in American Christendom, we think too much like the disciples of old. We have a dream for our life, but that dream can't compare to what God has planned. Like the original disciples, we tend to focus so much on our own zip code, and God blessing our own household, that we forget God calls, commands, and commissions us to be a blessing to others. It just may be that God's plan for your life is far greater than you think—and His capacity to do monumental things in and through our life is truly incomparable!

Everything God has for us is worth the wait.

We aren't fans of waiting, because we live in a culture of immediate gratification. More than the old adage "Good things come to those who wait," God invites us into His process. Everything God has for us is worth the wait. Though we struggle with an aversion to process, whatever God has promised will also be worth whatever process is required.

We have a high and holy privilege to be the Noahs, Abrams, Moseses, and Elijahs of our day and age. May we not have to experience Acts 8:1 in order to be obedient to Acts 1:8. God doesn't desire us to be stuck or to settle. Take it from Terah, Abram's father: Don't get stuck. Don't settle. As a young minister named Luke LeFevre so eloquently put it, "Don't die in Haran!"

Altars (The Conference)

In January 2025, Kelly and I attended a conference in New York City called "Altars." I wasn't familiar with the church hosting it or many of the people on the platform; however, I heard some timely spiritual encouragement from guys like Pastor Jon Tyson, Pastor Corey Russell, and Pastor Luke LeFevre. Full disclosure: Luke's message was so profound to me, as I was neck deep in writing this book, that I *knew* I had to talk about his message here somewhere.

As soon as he said, "Turn to Genesis 12," I leaned in and began to listen carefully. Talk about timing! The exact character, story, and subject matter I'd been writing about was the subject of his message that day at the conference. Though surrounded by three thousand strangers, I felt this word was surely for me. I can't say I was fully prepared for the spiritual bomb God would drop through this familiar Biblical character, as I thought I had a handle on his story, but He sure did. This young evangelist, Luke LeFevre, did a masterful job of painting a different side of the picture, encouraging me, and allowing God to speak to me on the subject I've written about for you! For that next thirty minutes or so, God would strongly confirm that my trip to New York for this conference was nothing short of providential. It was evident that God took us to Altars so that I could pass on to you the encouragement He gave to me:

- Don't get stuck—keep moving forward in faith.
- Grief is unavoidable, but don't let it become a god in your life.
- Yes, there will come mountains and storms and giants.
- Don't settle for anything less than God's movement and God's calling!
- And, as Pastor Luke said, *don't die in Haran.*

Before diving into Genesis 12, Pastor Luke actually invited us to back up and look at Abram's dad, Terah. Let's consider Genesis 11:31 (NLT):

One day Terah took his son Abram, his daughter-in-law Sarai [his son Abram's wife], and his grandson Lot [his son Haran's child] and moved away from Ur of the Chaldeans. He was headed for the land of Canaan, but they stopped at Haran and settled there.

If we aren't careful, we can read this little story about a seemingly insignificant character named Terah and miss the point altogether. There are some powerful truths here that are worthy of examination. Backing up a few verses from verse 31, we gather more information.

Terah's Story

Terah had three sons—Abram, Nahor, and Haran—with Haran being the youngest. Here's what we read about them in Genesis 11:27–32 (NLT):

This is the account of Terah's family line. Terah became the father of Abram, Nahor and Haran. And Haran became the father of Lot. While his father Terah was still alive, Haran died in Ur of the Chaldeans, in the land of his birth.

Abram and Nahor both married. The name of Abram's wife was Sarai, and the name of Nahor's wife was Milkah; she was the daughter of Haran, the father of both Milkah and Iskah. Now Sarai was childless because she was not able to conceive.

—

Don't settle for anything less than God's movement and God's calling!

Terah took his son Abram, his grandson Lot, son of Haran, and his daughter-in-law Sarai, the wife of his son Abram, and together they set out from Ur of the Chaldeans to go to Canaan. But when they came to Haran, they settled there.

Terah lived 205 years, and he died in Haran.

Terah's life didn't end up quite the way he most likely planned or hoped it would. Chances are as you've read this book, you have already realized that maybe your own life hasn't gone the way you planned or dreamed either.

Sarai, Abram's wife, couldn't have children, which was catastrophic in that culture because it meant no blessing and no heir. To add to that pain, now Terah had lost his youngest son to an untimely death. Given both the barrenness of his marriage and the loss of his brother Haran, Abram adopted one of Haran's offspring, Lot.

Haran's death, I believe, is critically important to the story. Terah most likely saw the birth of all three of his sons in Haran, and it was customary in that time to name offspring after important cities or geographical locations. However, at some point, Terah moved his family to Ur. We don't really know why, and there's no reason to speculate, since it's not important to the story. The point is that it's in Ur that Terah lost his son Haran. And while Scripture isn't clear as to why Terah would leave Ur, he at some point decided to take off with his remaining family toward Canaan, which would eventually become the land God promised to Abram. However, for some reason on the way, Terah stopped in Haran, and the Bible says he settled there and died. Most likely gripped by the pain of grief, Terah didn't make it to Canaan.

Could it be that Terah built an altar to his pain? Could it be that the pain of losing so much caused him to stop moving forward? How many times have we revisited a memory of something painful and life-altering, as if on repeat, that we got stuck in that moment—as Bono of U2 says, "stuck in a moment that you can't get out of"? Painful, life-altering experiences can incapacitate us and render us unable to move forward in faith, because we get stuck in our sorrow. It's okay to grieve the life you thought you'd have; just be careful not to settle for it and get stuck in it.

Move Past That Moment

The grip of grief may very well have caused Terah to stop and settle in Haran. We know at one time Terah was a polytheist. However, Pastor Luke challenged us to reflect: "What if, just imagine, what if God originally was calling Terah to be the father of faith, before calling Abram?"

In spite of such great pain, what if God was calling Terah to move past that grief and step into a greater life and greater promise? I mean, he did take off with his family toward Canaan! That sounds familiar, doesn't it? Except, unlike Abram, Terah got stuck along the way there and settled in a land bearing the name of his greatest loss.

What if he couldn't get past his altar of pain to allow it to propel him into a monumental purpose? Don't hear that as insensitive, but intentional. Don't you want God to take the broken parts of your life and redeem, restore, and resurrect new life? Don't you want beauty from ashes and joy from mourning?

There are so many undeserving altars we bow before and wrongly give our attention and affection. We spend so much of our time on lesser gods when the God of the universe patiently, gracefully, and lovingly waits for us, whispering His divine invitation to a destiny we could never imagine for ourselves.

We will endure hardships in this life that are too great for us, and we'll need God to move through them or past them. Likewise, God's assignment for our lives will be too great for us, and we'll need God to enable us to fulfill it.

—

It's not God's assignment if you don't need God to accomplish it.

You can bet it's not God's assignment if you don't need God to accomplish it. However, the path of God's assignment will not be free of suffering, sifting, storms, giants, or grief. The path toward a monumental life and living your created purpose will come with moments of crushing, but take heart: The greatest of our crushings unleashes even greater measures of anointing. What the enemy meant for evil, God will work for our good and His glory. Amen.

Noah, Abraham, Moses, Jacob, Job, Paul, Terah—Jesus. No matter who you look at in the Scriptures, there is always a measure of suffering that enables them to walk in God's authority and anointing. It may be that the monumental life God has planned for you requires the crushing because your assignment will require a great anointing.

Again, as strange as it sounds, be encouraged:

- It was the crushing of Jesus that allowed the anointing of the Holy Spirit upon Jesus's people.
- It was Abram allowing the crushing of his old life and old dreams that allowed him to be anointed for *God's* assignment and dream.

And not to put myself in the class of these faith heroes at all, but it was quite possibly the crushing of my childhood church experience that set up an anointing for my future assignment.

God Uses Everything (Nothing Is Wasted)

We don't get olive oil until the olives are crushed, and we don't get anointing without parts of our lives being crushed either. We have to let the altars of pain become altars of praise because it's the God of all creation who is with us, for us, working, and doing something. We may not be able to see what He's doing today, but we can trust Him in faith for our tomorrows. It could well be that the current crushing is opening the door for a new anointing.

—

We may not be able to see what He's doing today, but we can trust Him in faith for our tomorrows.

Rest assured, when it comes to God, nothing is wasted. He can and will use anything and redeem everything along the path to our purpose. I could have remained stuck, letting the hurt from my church experience debilitate me and metaphorically dying in the Haran of my rejection. In fact, I nearly did, *but God.*

When faced with the overflowing Jordan River, the Israelites could have chosen to get stuck and settled, embracing unbelief, even after God had proven Himself time and time again. What if the "Jordan River moments" of our lives are really leading us to freedom after a long season of waiting or adversity?

We must be careful not to abdicate our assignment by allowing the crushing to incapacitate us. We've seen that in the Scripture as well. As we saw in the last chapter, Elijah witnessed a supernatural moment when God shot literal fire down from heaven at the showdown with Baal. There's another part of the story we didn't explore. It wasn't long after that epic duel that Jezebel, the demonized witch, frightened Elijah so much that he ran away.

How did we go from showdown to meltdown so fast? Elijah had just seen the power of God on full display. It was hundreds against one, and God moved on his behalf. But then, facing one evil woman, he ran away? God gave him a few opportunities to correct his course, to no avail.

Not long after, God seemingly moved on, telling Elijah to prepare his replacement, Elisha. God had a plan, and if Elijah wouldn't cooperate, is it possible that God called his apprentice to take over the assignment? Did Elijah just abdicate his assignment out of fear?

We can't settle. We can't get scared. We must choose faith over fear.

Too much is at stake to get stuck.

Don't die in Haran.

The Words "Abdicate" & "Assignment" Don't Belong Together

Could it be that, like Elijah and Elisha, God chose to skip over Terah? Did Terah abdicate a holy assignment, causing God to move on to Abram?

Then we see Abraham (the artist formerly known as Abram), take his son of promise, Isaac, up on a mountain of sacrifice to worship. Could this be another story within a greater story? It's as if God invited Abraham to a potential altar of pain, asking him to sacrifice his son, his heir, his blessing—the one he had waited and prayed for, the one who would be the very root of His promise of descendants. Again, don't miss the foreshadowing of the greater story being told!

Pastor Luke set the scene and summed up God's riveting question to Abraham: "Will you settle here, like your dad, and die too, if your son dies as well, Abraham?"

You could sense the collective gut punch in the room, as all three thousand of us in attendance felt that question deep down.

We briefly talked about King Saul in chapter 5. Saul disobeyed God and ended up building a monument to himself. His disobedience and pride caused God to remove His hand from King Saul, thus removing the anointing and the assignment, which caused the king to live in torment. Could this be why David prayed the way he prayed to God in Psalm 51, after his sin had been called out and exposed?

David knew from a young age that God had removed the anointing from King Saul and placed it upon him, yet David served Saul faithfully until it was his appointed time. There are many things we can learn from this story about assignment, anointing, and appointing; still, the primary thing I hope you see is that David knew what it looked like when God removed authority, assignment, and anointing. So, when the prophet Nathan later rebuked David in 2 Samuel 12 due to his grave sin, David responded very differently than Saul had.

In King David, we see that the mercy of God brings conviction, and David responds accordingly. Unlike Saul, who got stuck due to his pride and his all-too-willing choice to linger in his sin, David quickly embraces a posture of brokenness and repentance, as he pleads with God not to take His Spirit from him. David did not want to repeat the pride-filled sin of Saul and risk the anointing, authority, or assignment of God being removed from his life! David's swift, humble response forever marked him as a man after God's heart.

This is a powerful example for us regarding the proper posture before a holy God—especially when we have drifted from our God-appointed destiny to fulfill some sort of fleshly desire.

Here's the point.

We can't abdicate our anointing, authority, or assignment. Far too much is at stake! We can't let our hurt or offense cause us to build altars of pain that keep us from an altar of praise. As hard as it has been or may become, we must trust the Lord for His provision as we are on His path and process.

Nothing God does is wasted. Everything God does or allows, He uses for our preparation and purpose. Remember, God works all things together for our good and for His glory. On our journey, for our assignment, God will use the crushing to bring new levels of anointing and authority. Though we may not understand it or see right away, God has a funny way of moving mountains by allowing us to face the giants.

Don't settle. Don't get stuck. Don't abdicate. Nothing is wasted.

Terah was 205 years old when he finally died. It's as if God gave him opportunity after opportunity, for years. God gave Elijah opportunity after opportunity before moving on to Elisha. God has given His people opportunity after opportunity to correct their course, and God gives you and me opportunity after opportunity as well. He has a plan, and He will always make a way.

The Good News Is...

If we are still breathing, God isn't finished with us yet. He is still giving us opportunities to course-correct. He is still inviting us into His plan for our life and His purposes. He is still inviting us to make sense of the pains of this life for our good and for His glory.

—

We can't abdicate our anointing, authority, or assignment. Far too much is at stake!

If you aren't dead, He's not done. We've heard that, sung that, and seen that on reels—because it's true. Keep moving forward in faith. Don't get stuck. Don't settle. Turn your altars of pain into altars of praise. Don't abdicate your assignment. God has a monumental life planned just for you. You are unique—the one and only you there will ever be.

Embrace the cross and the crushing, because that is where you will find the anointing and authority for your assignment. See any pain you may face in your life as providential, as strange as that may sound, and realize God works in mysterious ways. Again, I'd remind you of the words of A.W. Tozer, who said, "It is doubtful that God can bless a man greatly until He hurts him deeply."

You may feel like you've been laboring, working, waiting, praying, seeking, suffering, and searching, but the number seven matters.

Don't Stop at Six

Consider Jericho.

You may feel like you've been marching for days. Trusting in faith for God to move. The walls didn't fall the first six times around. You're tired and, honestly, doubting.

I'll never forget hearing Pastor Steven Furtick preach on this when he paused dramatically and said, "Don't stop at six!"

What a powerful and profound statement. "Don't stop at six! Go the full, complete seven." There is a power in the seventh time around. Walls fall when you proceed in faith. Even though you're tired, keep marching. Keep moving. Don't stop. Don't settle. Don't get stuck. Don't die in Haran. Keep moving forward in faith.

God is on the move, inviting you into a deep, meaningful, and monumental life.

God has an incredible plan for your life. He is calling you to a monumental purpose—to live as a memorial to His power, His greatness, His kindness, His goodness, His faithfulness. God wants to use you for His glory, and whatever He does is good. He can turn whatever is painful in your life into a reason to praise Him. He created you on purpose and for purpose, and there is nothing accidental in what He does, nothing wasted.

Don't stop at six. Don't allow yourself to get stuck. Don't settle for being a spectator on the park benches and die in Haran. God is on the move, inviting you into a deep, meaningful, and monumental life, in which He is with you every step of the way. Be encouraged by the words of Paul in Philippians 1:6 (NLT), which says, "I am certain that God, who began the good work within you, will continue his work until it is finally finished on the day when Christ Jesus returns."

Keep going—it'll be worth it in the end. Throw yourself into the work of the Master, confident that nothing you do for Him is a waste of time or effort.

Pray this prayer with me:

Jesus, give me the grace and strength to release and forgive any altars of pain, allowing them to become altars of praise. If I'm stuck or settling, help me not to abdicate any assignment from You, but rather to embrace whatever crushing has come so that I may be fully aware and alive in the fresh oil of Your anointing. I desire deeply to be Your living stone, Your monument, a Spirit-filled memorial to Your Name. Give me the perspective I need today to get up, pick up my mat, and begin walking in resurrection power. And Father, please hear me declare these seven words boldly and with great faith: **I don't want to die in Haran.** Take my life and use it to the fullest, for the fullness of Your plans and purposes, for Your glory alone. I pray this in Your Name, Jesus. Amen.

CONCLUSION

STACK THOSE STONES

2 Peter 1:12–15 (NLT)

Therefore, I will always remind you about these things—even though you already know them and are standing firm in the truth you have been taught. And it is only right that I should keep on reminding you as long as I live. For our Lord Jesus Christ has shown me that I must soon leave this earthly life, so I will work hard to make sure you always remember these things after I am gone.

Final Words

Hebrews 1 says faith shows the reality we hope for; it is the evidence of things we cannot see. If we don't see it before we see it, we'll never see it. The fathers of old earned their reputation through their faith, and I'd offer that God's reputation was also made known through their actions and steps of faith. These faith fathers and mothers were examples for all to look to, and they remain monumental examples today!

As we established at the very beginning of this book, God creates every person *on* purpose and *for* purpose, including *you*! Our lives have deep meaning, genuinely matter, and will represent something. We were born for significance and every single one of us has a story to tell. God points to us as His examples, according to Ephesians. May we live unto God like those who have come before us. May the life we live and the legacy we plan to leave behind be like that of Abel, as we see in Hebrews 1:4. It was by faith that Abel brought a more acceptable offering to God than Cain did. What a powerful prize to live, desiring and pursuing, so that long after we are dead, our story will still speak because of our example of faith.

—

God points to us as His examples.

— Ephesians 2:7 (paraphrased)

I want to leave you with this exhortation:

- Remember *who* you are. You are the *Imago Dei.* You are created in His image and carry His DNA in your identity.
- Remember *whose* you are. You are bought with a price and redeemed because of God's relentless love for you. You are not your own any longer; you belong to Jesus!
- Remember *what* you are called to be. You are a living stone, a now acceptable sacrifice, an instrument, and a memorial to His miracles. You are seated in a place of priority, and God points to your life as a declaration of who He is. Simply by nature of who your heavenly Father is, you have a powerful and profound purpose and part to play in His story.

I implore you to embrace these truths. Engage in this abundant, monumental life that God has designed just for you. Start right now, today. It's never too late. Hear me when I say, if you have breath in your lungs, then you have purpose in your life. God is inviting you to live your life on mission as a memorial, a monument, standing on the miraculous foundation of His powerful miracles to joyfully and faithfully represent His goodness, greatness, and glory.

This is the monumental life: choosing to live as an instrument, a living monument, His living stone, offered as a holy and pleasing aroma to the Lord. Embracing God's desires and design for your life will bless this world more than any talent you may possess or any accomplishment you may be acknowledged for. The only achievement that genuinely matters is a heart that is passionately offered to the Lord and a faithful obedience to God's assignments. Again, it's not about accumulating wealth, status, followers, etc. It's about Jesus and Jesus alone!

It's always been about Jesus, it will always be about Jesus, and long after we are gone, it will still simply be all about Jesus!

What could happen if, from this day forward, you committed your every step to be a seed? What could happen if you were to take those seemingly small yet faith-filled, significant steps, day by day, hour by hour, moment by moment, in the same direction? Could the spiritual plates shift? Could a tsunami of God's glory begin to move?

What if God called us in such a way that we too could make a profound impact like Edward Kimball? Imagine if God gave you a glimpse into the type of indelible, eternal impact your life could have by walking intimately with Him in obedience? What if God revealed to you the difference your life could make by embracing the monumental life He dreamed for you long ago?

How amazing would it be at some point, when our faith is made sight, if the Lord showed us the harvest that happened in the wake of our faithfulness?

—

God points to your life as a declaration of who He is.

Oh, God, our prayer is that You would allow the fullness of our lives to become a glory-filled tidal wave that, in some way, brings revival to this world. What an incredible thought, but more so, what an incredible privilege that the God of all creation calls us His own and invites us to live this abundant, monumental life He planned for us long before He spoke anything into existence.

Press On

As we pray and move forward in faith, we must remember that we will face many seasons throughout our journey with God when we feel the shifting and the sifting. Moments will come when it will be imperative that we return to those stacks of stones, look back, and remember. When hardships become more than you can handle, that is your signal to lean into God, walk trusting His Spirit, and return to those Ebenezers to remind yourself of the fidelity of God. The God of goodness who has been so incredibly and generously faithful in the past will be faithful today.

On the path to our God-designed destiny, there will come seasons of pruning and sifting when we will desperately need to recall His goodness and kindness in our past. Pruning is painful, but those stacked stones, those moments revisited, will remind us that God's not punishing us—rather, He's growing us and preparing us to possess His next promise.

God is writing a greater story through your life, and it is a story of legacy.

Those miracle moments memorialized will be a constant reminder that His presence is with us in the pruning and purging times. As we become living monuments through the seasons of shifting and sifting, we will point to a good, holy, powerful, and able God as an example to others.

Whatever discomfort we may face simply indicates new oil coming, likely for the next season that He invites us to step into. As it was when God reminded His people in the days of Isaiah, I believe it is today.

Consider Isaiah 43:16–19 (NLT):

"I am the Lord, who opened a way through the waters, making a dry path through the sea. I called forth the mighty army of Egypt with all its chariots and horses. I drew them beneath the waves, and they drowned, their lives snuffed out like a smoldering candlewick. But forget all that—it is nothing compared to what I am going to do, for I am about to do something new. See, I have already begun! Do you not see it? I will make a pathway through the wilderness. I will create rivers in the dry wasteland."

In this passage, God reminds His people to remember His faithfulness, as He made a way for them through the Red Sea and the Jordan River. He has always been a God of doing something new. He is the God who is unfathomably able.

He is the same God today. No matter what may come in this life, our God will always create pathways through any wilderness we may find ourselves wandering through. He can and will create rivers of life in any barren, dry wasteland we encounter.

With this assurance in mind, why would we, as God's chosen people, ever struggle with any sense of insecurity, fear, or doubt? We serve at the pleasure of a God who has given us everything imaginable to feel secure.

Back to How We Began

I asked at the beginning of this book, and I'll ask at the end: What if I told you that one small step, which may seem insignificant in your eyes, could be the catalyst to change the world? What if I told you that now is *your* time, and God is inviting you to take a step of faith that could lead to a life like you've never imagined for yourself?

The steps you choose to take, intentionally or unintentionally, will make a mark in some way. You will have an impact on many people. Your life is significant because you were created for significance by a supernatural and significant God. God is writing a greater story through your life, and it is a story of legacy.

What is God's vision for your life? If you don't begin to see it in faith before you see it in fruition, sadly, you'll never see it at all. That would be a great tragedy.

So build a life that is a monument to His faithfulness.

Build for legacy, with future generations in mind, so they won't forget.

Build in a way that declares His greatness and His goodness.

Stack each stone to mark and memorialize the miraculous way that God has proven Himself repeatedly as your shepherd, source, protector, and provider.

He has been, and will remain, faithful through the wind and waves.

He has been, and will remain, faithful in the seasons of suffering.

He has been, and will remain, faithful.

Made for This Moment

So, what is God inviting you to join Him in doing? What is the assignment? What does this monumental life look like that He is calling you to, and created you for? It could feel like a Jericho or a Nineveh, but I assure you, with God, it's a Canaan.

It could feel like a Jericho or a Nineveh, but I assure you, with God, it's a Canaan.

Much like Elijah prophesying rain, we must learn to discern God's voice to hear Him speak. We must learn to discern how God operates so that we can operate with Him. Unless we determine what He is asking of us in the Spirit, we may never see His abundant, monumental plans come to fruition. Let's also keep in mind that we may never see the fullness of God's plan come to fruition on this side of heaven. That is okay! Still, we must continue to move with Him to where He leads.

The spiritual seeds we plant along the path may be for trees we never see, but remember Edward Kimball, whose steps of faith led to a global awakening. He died at age seventy-seven, and no, that number presenting itself again doesn't surprise me.

Remember, Kimball led D.L. Moody to the Lord seventy-nine years before Billy Graham came to know Jesus, and he would die thirty-three years before Billy Graham came to know Jesus. Kimball would never live to see the global harvest from the seeds he planted and steps of faith he chose to take generations prior. When we are encouraged to plant spiritual seeds of faith for trees we may never see, let's trust and believe that the harvest will come.

God knew exactly what He was doing when He created Edward Kimball and called him to his assignment. It's as if Kimball couldn't help himself. His heart had been so arrested by the reality of Jesus that he couldn't do anything other than emphatically say *yes* to God's design and desires for his life.

Elijah too, so enraptured by the reality of God and choosing to walk with God in faith, prophesied rain because he heard God say rain would come. He saw it in the Spirit months before he saw a single cloud in the sky. We can't stop believing God when all we see is a drought. Elijah went back up to the mountain, where he'd seen God so faithfully and powerfully move, and he remembered His greatness. There, he prayed, continued to believe, and searched the skies for a cloud beginning to swell! He prayed and sought *seven times*, knowing God would eventually move. The plates would shift. The tsunami would crash against the shores. The mountain would form.

There's so much about Edward Kimball and the prophet Elijah that reveals a significant call, anointing, and assignment from God. The same could be said of us when we step in faith and obedience! Much like Queen Esther, I believe you were made for this moment, but be patient in the process. Allow God to build within you what will be necessary for all He desires to do through you.

Kimball would never live to see the millions of people flooding altars; however it was through his passionate faith that a global awakening eventually came to fruition.

David continued to be a shepherd boy for a while, in waiting, even after he knew God had an assignment and an anointing for him that would one day change the world.

Jesus waited until He was thirty before moving into His ministry. It's not that the mission and mandate weren't there; He just waited for His appointed time.

Be faithful in the waiting, because it's in the waiting that God does His best work. Faith requires dying to our need and desire for immediate gratification. We must place that mindset upon the altar. Deny the lie that we aren't doing something significant if we can't see it for ourselves. Trust God when He says rain will come, even though there are no clouds in the sky.

The Monumental Moment

There's a television series that Amazon Prime released called *House of David*, which provides a fascinating perspective on King David's story. Though it takes some creative license, the series is both powerful and beautiful. There's a particular scene that moved me, in season 1, episode 8, part 2. David comes before the king, whom he would eventually replace, to request the king's permission to fight the giant Goliath, who had everyone else gripped in fear.

A few of David's brothers try to remove him from the king's presence so he won't say anything that could get him in trouble, but David, resolute, boldly requests permission to fight on behalf of the king. As the brothers quickly try to drag David out of the tent, King Saul says, "Let him speak!"

Be faithful in the waiting, because it's in the waiting that God does His best work.

Here, David humbly approaches the king and says, "My king, I will fight the giant."

Saul knows David because it was David who soothed Saul from his torment by singing. "You are only a boy, and you cannot fight him," the king says, with a look of compassion and trust.

David then mounts a defense, recounting the dangers of faithfully keeping his father's sheep for years and having to fight off lions and bears. Then, with fierce passion, he gets on one knee, humbly imploring King Saul, "This giant blasphemes the Lord of Hosts, but the same Lord who rescued me from the lion and the bear will rescue me from the hand of this Philistine."

With compassion in his eyes, Saul gently replies, "That monster is a man of war. He was made for this."

Then comes the most gripping moment in the episode.

—

He's built a monument—His very own people!

Before King Saul even finishes his sentence, David, with the confidence of heaven and fire in his eyes, says, "I was made for this—for this moment. Trust me, my king. I will slay this giant."

I couldn't help but be overcome with emotion, because as it just so happened, I was in the midst of writing the book's conclusion when I watched this episode. That moment in that show made me think of you.

God has created and called you, inviting you to embrace His design and desire for your life. With every fiber of my being, I believe that God has a significant purpose for you and has been preparing you for such a time as this. There may be some process yet to come. You may still endure some painful storms and situations, but know that God is inviting you on the path toward His promise for you, and He is with you. His plans and purposes are extraordinary, indelible, and monumental.

As We Go

With all this said, as we go, I want to leave you where we began in the introduction, with the very first verse I mentioned, Psalm 148:13–14 (MSG): *"Let them praise the Name of God—it's the only Name worth praising. His radiance exceeds anything in earth and sky; He's built a monument—His very own people!"*

That is *you*.

You are His person.

You are His monument.

You were made for this.

This is your monumental moment.

In His Name, by His power, and for His glory, rise up in faith!

Take the step.

Remove any obstacle to your obedience.

Slay the giants.

—

You were made for this. Be the monument.

Endurance will be essential.

Be that offering, that monument—that matters.

Be the stones that cry out, even if no one else will.

Don't settle for the park benches, spectating as others live into God's significant purposes—and don't die in Haran. You can't imagine what God will do in and through your steps of faith and faithfulness. All praise, honor, and glory be unto Him and Him alone. It will all be worth it!

Embrace the life God has designed and desires for you.

Be the monument.

My prayer for you:

Jesus, I pray for this faithful and faith-filled follower whom You deeply love and have incredible desires and design for. I pray for them, for the courage, strength, provision, and anointing for the assignments You have in mind and are calling them to. Father, I know with You there are no accidents, just as I know that nothing is wasted. You have uniquely created this person as one of one. There is none other in all of Your created world who is like them, so Jesus, I pray for You to guard them in Your grace and kindness, and fill them with Your holy fire. I pray for an even greater measure of faith in the days to come, as they take steps with You and embrace the monumental life You have for them. Lastly God, I pray for Your protection, peace, provision, and prosperity in all they do, that You will confirm the work of their hands, and that You will give them the desires of their heart! Use them, I pray, Jesus, may they now rise up in Your Name, by Your power, and for Your glory, as You leverage every part of their lives as a monument which memorializes Your goodness and greatness! All of this, I pray, in Your holy, powerful, magnificent, and wonderful Name, Jesus. Amen.

ACKNOWLEDGMENTS OF SOME MONUMENTS IN MY LIFE

Extra special thanks to my mom, Sharon Sherrill, a monument deserving of a whole book to herself. Mom, you and Dad have led by example, taking the long journey in the same direction, step by step, faithfully walking with God. I thank God for you and love you! Your life, and marriage, are monuments of grace to me.

Dad and Dedy, your life and love for Jesus has left a monumental legacy in our family. You are both so deeply missed, but we know your faith has been made sight.

Also, special thanks to my family: my first hero, my big sister Stacy, as well as Scott, Brayden, Britton, Pops, Joyce, Keith, Lanay, Emily, Luke, Warren, Gail, Kathy, Richard, David, Michael, and all our extended family. Kel and I are so thankful for you each and love you all.

Thank you to Nick "Kenly" James for being the daughter we never had and for always trying to keep me in check, making sure things run smoothly at Reach and 220!

James and Caroline Roberts: What a journey we've been on, huh? Here's to the next fifty years!

Mark and Nicole Odom, you were the first to sign on, and I have a feeling no matter what, you'll be with us till the end. #ShOTime!

To some special families who have walked with us, prayed for us, and supported us in immeasurable ways over the years: Greg and Sherry Webster and family, Allen and Doris Tarbutton, Curtis and Traci Samford and family, Drew and Julia Kronenberger, Larry and Jessie Gustine, Dennis and Patty Shumate, and Barry & Fran Blanton.

Brita, thank you for keeping Kelly and me sane and organized! I agree that I am far more challenging than Kelly on this task. You are deeply appreciated! Aaron, you are truly an "Aaron" in EVERY way. Thank you for your faithful, loyal friendship. I always know you are praying and believing for the best! You are my radical faith friend ... EVERY time! :)

Jeff Miller, your coaching, guiding, editing, and banter have made all the difference in the world! Thank you, and let's do this again? Nicole, thanks for always being willing to help edit all of my crazy, along with my ellipses habit. Krista, thanks for being a beta reader and believing in this project so deeply. Allen, Doris, Dan, RuAnne, and Colin Millar, thank you for praying and believing.

To my pastors, Jeff Wells and Ken Werlein: You embody the message of monuments and inspire me to be a better lover of Jesus and people. I respect, admire, and pray to be the pastor you both are!

To our Declaration Family. You humble me, inspire me, and Kelly and I are so honored to be your pastors. We love you with all our hearts. To our Elder families, Mike and Krista Rollins, Alan and Tabitha Gathuru, Mark and Nicole Odom, Keith and Tiffany Guenther, Drew and Julia Kronenberger, and Donald and Cathy Borucki: Kelly and I are honored to walk, serve, and lead with you. Scott and Courtney Nickel, we miss you guys! Come home.

Special thanks to our entire staff team at Declaration—what an honor to walk and work beside you! We are thankful for you and love you. The best is yet to come!

To the 220 Leadership Team, Nick James, Kevin and Sara Jones, James and Caroline Roberts, Meredith Haynes, JD and Allison Humber, Jadon & Chloe Sherrill, Zac and Lesleigh Zimmerman, Toby and Jana Foreman, Chelsea Peper, Blaine and Tiffany St. Germain, and Jeff and Leanne Brady: We've stacked many stones together—and here's to many more!

Thank you to my band mates: The OGs (Kevin Jetton and Curtis Willliams), Seth Johnson, Josh Smith (maestro), Craig Weaver, Dave Keil, Zack Jones, Charlie McCrae, Jacob Lampley, and Lesleigh

Zimmerman. What an honor to have led with you all these years. Also, Kyle Lee (My favorite producer and co-writer), your gift and anointing never ceases to amaze me.

Phil -Z- Conner, my friend, my brother. I'm so thankful for that first youth camp at Alto Frio. Since then, you have been one of my greatest champions and most faithful friend, and I'm deeply grateful to you.

Rick Eubanks, Aubrey Spears, Ross King, you inspire me, encourage me, and make me want to follow Jesus with even more passion.

Tim Ramsey, thank you for seeing something in me long ago and calling it out. I am thankful for you, my friend.

Larry York, thank you for showing me who and what a pastor is supposed to really look like, long ago. I'm deeply thankful for your belief and pursuit of me.

Dr. Scott Stripling and Dr. Israel Steinmetz, thank you for pushing me beyond my comfort zone and instilling a different type of hunger in me.

Also, thank you so much to some of our friends and amazing co-laborers: John and Sandy Hines, Kyle and Shelly Lee, Cas and Gina Webster, Jacob and Francesca Lampley, Aubrey and Janielle Spears, Brian and Jessica Arrendell, Greg and Yvonne Johnson, Joe and Emily McShane, Stephen and Meredith Alfred, Paul and Shannon Broadbent, Stephen McDonald, Daniel and Melody Gathright, Blake & Krystle Quimby, Gregg & Kelly Matte, Brandon & Shauna Maness, Chad & Jeanne Hays, Jeff & Emily Hays, Daniel "Critter" & Melissa Crittendon, Jake Kelfer and team, Julie Bullock, Doug & Julie Crozier, Josh & Erin Means, Dave and Tara DiFrancesca, Josh and Kara Joines, Scot and Liza Pollok, and Mark and Sandy Moreno, Kelly and I are privileged to serve Jesus and live life with you all.

Halle girl, you are special, and God has such incredible plans and dreams for you. It's an honor to walk with you and watch God move in and through your life!

Lastly, to every student, adult, and generous donor over the past 25 years who have been a part of the 220 Conference:

Remember who you are.
Remember WHOSE you are.
Remember what you are called to be.

You are a monument that HE is building, His very own people.

You are a generation rising!

In His Name.
By His Power.
For His Glory.

ABOUT THE AUTHOR

John Sherrill is a pastor, author, worship leader, and communicator with a passion for helping people encounter the presence of God. Known for his vulnerability, honest storytelling, and deep biblical insight, he bridges timeless truth with real life—delivering messages filled with creativity, humor, and heart.

In Monuments, John draws from personal trials and family stories to explore surrender, purpose, and God's enduring faithfulness. His words challenge readers to move beyond fear and insecurity and build lives of eternal impact that stand as lasting testaments to Christ.

John and his wife, Kelly, lead Declaration Church in North Houston, where they love helping families discover freedom, purpose, and a faith that endures.

Find John online: johnsherrill.com | @johnsherrill

WHAT OTHERS ARE SAYING

"I have known John Sherrill a long time. He is a pastor who not only cares about people, but he is also deep with God. He has written a superb book that is at once honest, challenging, and encouraging! You will enjoy it, and you will grow closer to Jesus!"

— Jeff Wells
Lead Pastor, WoodsEdge Community Church
The Woodlands, TX

"I've sung John Sherrill's songs and shared the stage with him at Breakaway Ministries and student camps many times. Now I'm thrilled his pen has moved from lyrics to chapters. In these pages, he offers hard-won wisdom forged through challenge, prayer, and Scripture, delivered with the same honest heart that shaped his music. Monuments is clear, practical, and deeply encouraging. Let my friend John encourage and guide you toward the monumental life God-designed just for you."

— Gregg Matte
Pastor of Houston's First Baptist Church
Founder of Breakaway Ministries

"John Sherrill writes like he pastors - with a rare blend of grace and truth that both penetrates and inspires. As someone who has faithfully served in the trenches of ministry for years, John brings the wisdom of a tried-and-true pastor, the heart of a worship leader, and the authenticity of a man who lives what he preaches. This isn't theory from an ivory tower; it's truth forged in the realities of leading a congregation, raising a family, and walking daily with God. Chapter 9 alone is worth the price of the book—I finished it ready to get up and run. If you're looking for a voice that will challenge and encourage you in equal measure, John Sherrill is that voice."

— Ken Werlein
Founding Pastor, Faithbridge Church
Spring, TX

"In Monuments, John Sherrill simultaneously demonstrates his vulnerability and his brilliance. The former lowers the reader's guard, allowing the latter to sketch a monumental faith journey. I love this book."

— Scott Stripling, PhD
The Bible Seminary, Provost
Near East Archaeological Society, President

"With rare vulnerability and hard-won wisdom, John Sherrill, in his book Monuments, reveals the secret of the spiritual life: that true meaning isn't built by achievements, it's cultivated through everyday steps of simple faithfulness. Drawing on his own winding story and the memory of figures like Joshua, Moses, and Abraham, John makes this book itself a monument to the miracles that come on the other side of surrender."

— Greg Basch
Former Campus Leadership Pastor, Elevation Church
Leadership Coach & Church Strategist, GregBasch.com

"With warmth and personal testimony through seasons of trial and testing, Pastor John passionately invites you to surrender fully to the faithfulness of God. This book will encourage you to persevere and live out the finished work of Jesus Christ—reflecting His grace and truth for future generations to see and bear witness to."

— Paul Bergin
Teaching Pastor, The Belonging Co. Church
Nashville, TN

"Monuments is a timely and heartfelt call to remember what truly matters in life. With wisdom born from experience and humor that keeps you laughing along the way, John helps us see how God's faithfulness can turn the painful and even ordinary moments of life into enduring monuments of grace. This book will inspire, convict, and comfort anyone who desires to live with deeper purpose and lasting impact."

—Josh Joines
Lead Pastor, Faith Family Church
Pastoral Coach & Leadership Strategist, Cadency.org

"It's so clear to me that John's life is a life laid down. A monumental life is not built overnight - it comes as a result of many moments and years of faith and surrender - and that is exactly what is echoed throughout the pages of this book. John, a true worshipper, demonstrates that the adventure of following Jesus is worth the cost. Through authenticity, humor, and an abundance of scripture, John invites all of us into the glory of God's kingdom and the dignity of God's call."

—Josh Henry
Former Student Pastor, The Belonging Co. Church
Evangelist, Nashville, TN

"What if you started life today by dedicating every step to God? That question is the tipping point to living a monumental life. Monuments is a book about how to scale your life according to God's grand vision that He has in mind, just for you. Stop thinking small, stop being stuck. The bleachers are no place for the believer. It's time to get going. Life is too short to live small. John's writing is personal, warm, thought-provoking, and motivating, so lean in and listen. Let John help you trek the highs and lows of building a life momentum that leads to a monumental life. Read this book! You'll be glad you did."

— Dr. Dave Edwards
Pastor of 1:1 discipleship, Church Project.
Speaker and Author

"Monuments by John Sherrill is a powerful and deeply meaningful book, written in John's unmistakable conversational style that draws you in from the first page. The stories, questions, and prayers make it personal and Spirit-led, encouraging reflection on God's faithfulness in our lives.

I was especially moved by the story of his son, Kyle, who was born with severe health challenges, and the way John shared his family's journey with honesty and hope. Historical and biblical examples — from the Haystack Prayer Meeting to Edward Kimball and Abram — beautifully illustrate the call to live as "living monuments" of God's glory. The phrase "Don't die in Haran" is a striking reminder to keep moving forward in faith.

This book is a timely and encouraging guide to embracing your identity in Christ, walking in obedience, and living a life that points back to Him. Inspirational, practical, and heartfelt — Monuments is a must-read for anyone seeking to honor God through their life."

— Rick Eubanks
National Network of Youth Ministries
State Coordinator, Texas

"Every once in a while, a book comes along that everyone should read. This is that book. Pastor and author John Sherrill weaves the story of God together with his story to create this masterpiece called Monuments. If you are needing to be reminded of your calling, this book is for you. If you feel trapped in a painful season, this book is for you. You will be reminded that whatever moment you find yourself in, God has a plan for it, and he wants to use you as a monument for his glory. You were made for this moment!"

— Greg Johnson
Lead Pastor, Restoration Church Woodforest
Montgomery, TX

"John Sherrill lives what he writes. His love for Jesus, passion for people, and unwavering devotion to the call of God shine through every page of Monuments. This book isn't theory—it's testimony. John writes with the authenticity of a pastor, the heart of a worshiper, and the faith of a man who has walked through the fire and come out refined. His stories will move you, his insight will challenge you, and his faith will awaken something deep within you. If you're longing to live a life that truly matters—a life that points others to the greatness of God—read this book. It will stir your heart, strengthen your faith, and call you to build a life that stands as a monument to His glory."

—Jimn Kyles, Lead Pastor, Anchor Bend Church
Author of Unstuck & Unstoppable

"My friend John Sherrill wrote a book that's going to breathe faith and hope back into a lot of people. Monuments is a reminder that your life still matters to God—that every step, every scar, and every story can point back to His goodness. John doesn't just write about this... he's lived it. Monuments is a beautifully curated blend of storytelling and spiritual truth. If you've ever wondered whether your life really matters, this book will remind you that you are part of God's monument to His glory."

— Dave DiFrancesca
Lead Pastor, The Avenue Church

Made in the USA
Coppell, TX
14 June 2026

79787986R00111